VICTORIAN DAYS

American Kids in History™

VICTORIAN DAYS

Discover the Past with Fun Projects, Games, Activities, and Recipes

David C. King

John Wiley & Sons, Inc.

New York • Chichester • Weinheim • Brisbane • Singapore • Toronto

The publisher and the author have made every reasonable effort to ensure that the experiments and activities in this book are safe when conducted as instructed but assume no responsibility for any damage caused or sustained while performing the experiments or activities in the book. Parents, guardians, and/or teachers should supervise young readers who undertake the experiments and activities in this book.

Library of Congress Cataloging-in-Publication Data
King, David C.
      Victorian days: discover the past with fun projects, games,
  activities, and recipes / David C. King.
         p. cm.
  Includes bibliographical references.
  ISBN 0-471-33122-8 (alk. paper)
  1. New York (N.Y.)—Social life and customs—19th century—Study and teaching—
Activity programs Juvenile literature.
  2. United States—Social life and customs—19th century—Study and teaching—
Activity programs Juvenile literature.
  3. Children—New York (State)—New York—Social life and customs—19th century—
Study and teaching—Activity programs Juvenile literature.
  4. Children—United States—Social life and customs—19th century—Study and teaching—
Activity programs Juvenile literature.
  I. Title.
  F128.47.K49 2000
  306'.09747'1—dc21   99-15480
                                             CIP

Printed in the United States of America
10 9 8 7 6 5 4 3 2 1

ACKNOWLEDGMENTS

Special thanks to the many people who made this book possible, including: Kate C. Bradford,
Diana Madrigal, Diane Aronson, and the editorial staff of the Professional and Trade Division, John Wiley & Sons, Inc.;
Susan E. Meyer and the staff of Roundtable Press, Inc.; Marianne Palladino and Irene Carpelis of
Michaelis/Carpelis Design; Miriam Sarzin, for her copy editing, Sharon Flitterman-King and
Diane Ritch for craft expertise; Rona Tuccillo for picture research; Cheryl Kirk Noll for the drawings;
Steven Tiger, librarian, and the students of the Roe-Jan Elementary School, Hillsdale, New York;
and, for research assistance, the staff members of the Great Barrington Public Library,
the Atheneum (Pittsfield, Massachusetts), Old Sturbridge Village, and
the Farmers Museum, Cooperstown, New York. Historical photographs
courtesy of Dover Publications, Inc.

CONTENTS

VICTORIAN DAYS

INTRODUCTION

An Age of Change

Between 1850 and 1900, America grew and changed in remarkable ways. What had been a country of farms and small villages was becoming a modern nation of growing cities and booming industries. Factories equipped with powerful machines now produced almost everything people needed or wanted. Machines also speeded up farm work, so that fewer farm workers were producing far more food than ever before. Many young people could now choose to leave the farm for factory jobs and the greater excitement of city life.

This period of growth and change became known as the "Victorian Age," named after England's Queen Victoria. It was during her long reign, from 1837 to 1901, that England and the United States emerged as the world's first industrial and urban nations.

Never before had there been so much wealth or so many things to buy. Dozens of amazing new inventions were making life more comfortable and more fun. Americans were now enjoying such wonders as indoor plumbing, electric lights, telephones, and phonographs. Some daring inventors were even trying to develop a flying machine, while others tinkered with a device called the automobile.

The great wealth of Victorian days was not shared by everyone, however. The wealthiest families lived in elegant mansions staffed with servants, and middle-class families enjoyed a comfortable way of life. But large numbers of people lived in poverty. For them, the Victorian Age was a time of struggle and hardship.

Many of the poor were newcomers—immigrants from other countries, drawn to America as the land of freedom and opportunity. During the 1890s, nearly 9 million immigrants arrived, more than ever before in the nation's history. Many came from the non-English-speaking countries of Europe, such as Russia, Poland, and Italy. About half of the newcomers were poor and were forced to live in crowded, unhealthy slum buildings called tenements. Men, women, and even children as young as seven toiled long hours in factories for wages that were barely enough to live on.

In spite of the hard beginnings, even the poorest had hope in the future. One reason for hope was that free public education was available to all. Every immigrant family believed that the American dream of a better life would come true, if not for them, at least for their children.

The Kadinskys and the Hobarts

This book follows two families through the year 1893. The Kadinskys and the Hobarts were not real families, but their stories will show what life was like for a wealthy family and a poor immigrant family in New York City during the Victorian Age. Mary Kadinsky had just turned eleven when she and her family arrived in America late in 1892. It had taken them six weeks to travel by railroad and steamship from their village in Poland. As their ship steamed into New York Harbor, they were thrilled to see the towering Statue of Liberty, which had been completed just six years earlier. After going through the new immigration center on Ellis Island, they rode a ferryboat into the city.

The Kadinsky family faced many hardships in their new homeland. Because they had little money, they were forced to live in a tenement, where they were crowded into two small rooms on the fourth floor. Mary's father, Joseph, found work as a railroad laborer, helping to lay new train tracks. Even working twelve hours a day, however, Papa Kadinsky did not earn enough money for the family to live on. To earn more, Mary's mother, Stella, took in piecework, making paper flowers for a department store. Mary and her brother Carl, who had just turned six, helped make the flowers and often took care of their little sister Rose, who was four years old.

The Kadinskys were confident that their lives would improve if they kept working hard. Mama managed to save a few pennies every day from her flower work, and Papa began looking for a better job. They were also hopeful because Mary and Carl would soon be starting school, where they would begin to learn the skills they would need for life in America.

This book follows Mary Kadinsky and her family through the spring and summer of 1893, and the Hobart family through the autumn and winter.

Twelve-year-old William Hobart and his family had recently moved into a large brick house near New York's Central Park. William's father, Austin Hobart, was a successful businessman, the vice president of a railroad company. William's mother, Juliette Hobart, had been the first woman in her family to go to college, at a time when the daughters of most well-to-do families were educated at home. While it was not considered proper for a Victorian lady to work outside the home, Mrs. Hobart was active in several clubs, including one that campaigned for voting rights for women.

William and his sister Lucy, who was six, loved their new home, which had been built in 1892. The handsome four-story building had indoor plumbing and electric lights, which the family liked much better than the gas lamps of their old house. Mr. Hobart was the head of the family and made all the important decisions, but Mrs. Hobart managed the everyday affairs of the household. She planned meals with the cook, Mrs. Bentley, and gave directions to the other servants, including a parlor maid, an upstairs maid, and a nanny for Lucy, plus a coachman and a stable boy for the family's carriages and three horses.

William attended a private school a few blocks from their home. He planned to go to college, but his real goal was to be a scientist and inventor, like his hero, Alexander Graham Bell, the man who had invented the telephone in 1876. William's parents encouraged his ambition and let him build a small workshop in the basement.

The Projects and Activities

What would it be like to be a kid growing up in Victorian America? In this book, you'll do many of the activities kids like Mary Kadinsky and William Hobart might have enjoyed in 1893. You'll create Polish paper cutouts, follow a recipe for New York cheesecake, play games like Polish checkers, make decorations for a Victorian Christmas, and much more. You can complete the projects and activities with materials you probably have at home or at school, or that you can easily buy at very little cost. As you enjoy the projects, activities, recipes, and games, the past will come alive, and you'll discover what it was like to be an American kid in Victorian days.

CHAPTER ONE

Spring

After the Kadinsky family's first cold, raw winter in New York City, the warmer weather of spring made life more pleasant. They could now open the windows every day to remove the stuffiness caused by the coal stove they used for heating and cooking. They could also spend their few spare hours getting to know their neighborhood and meeting other Polish immigrants who lived near them.

The streets became even busier and noisier than they were during the winter months. The sidewalks were crowded with people talking, laughing, shouting and bargaining, their voices mixed with the calls of street vendors selling their wares from wagons and pushcarts. Although the Kadinskys heard many different languages, it was the familiar sounds of Polish that made them feel more at home. Mama discovered she could bargain with Polish shopkeepers, and Mary managed to find other children who spoke Polish.

HELPING AT HOME

Mama Kadinsky spent almost twelve hours a day making paper flowers. Mary helped whenever she had a few minutes, and she also helped by doing many household chores. She followed Mama's directions for spring cleaning and, with Carl's help, put the blankets and rag-stuffed mattresses on the fire escape to air out. Then she scrubbed the floors and washed the windows. The Kadinskys were fortunate that their tenement had indoor plumbing, even though eight families shared each bathroom. There was also a faucet in the hallway where Mary filled the wash buckets that she then heated on the coal stove.

Mary was also learning to help with the cooking. She found that some of the foods in America were very strange. She had never tasted things like pumpkin pie, watermelon, or bananas. For most of their meals, however, Mama could buy the same kinds of ingre-dients she had used in Poland. She started Mary out with simple recipes, like biscuits filled with sausage meat, and showed her how to make tasty desserts that cost only pennies, like one called cinnamon bread sticks.

PROJECT PAPER FLOWERS

People in different parts of the world have folded and cut paper into beautiful shapes for many centuries. Poland is one of the countries most famous for this art form. Paper art became even more popular in the later 1800s because machines began to make inexpensive paper in huge quantities.

Paper flowers can be easy and fun to make. The kind you'll be making are similar to the flowers you see covering floats in holiday parades. Make a bunch of the flowers and use them to decorate your room, a present, or something you own, such as a bicycle.

MATERIALS

several sheets of newspaper

2 6-inch pipe cleaners (green, or white colored with green marking pen) for each flower

ruler

4 sheets of 5-by-8-inch thin paper for each flower, in any color (tissue paper, wrapping paper, or origami paper work well)

scissors

1. Spread several sheets of newspaper on your work surface.

2. Place the 4 sheets of thin colored paper on top of each other. Fold in about ½-inch of the 5-inch side of the stack. Turn the stack over and make a second ½-inch fold. Continue turning and folding to form a fan- or accordian fold, as shown in the drawing.

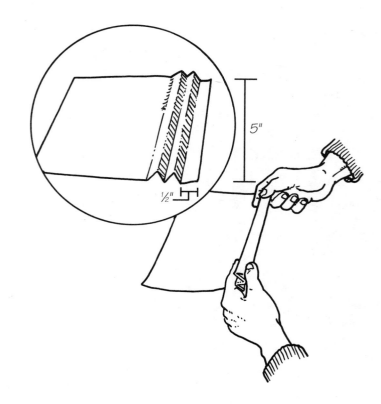

Tenement Sweat Labor

Many poor people worked in their tenement apartments, rather than in factories. They rolled cigars, made lace or paper flowers, sewed clothing, and performed other tasks. They learned to work hard and fast because they were paid not by the hour, but by how many pieces they completed. Known as piecework, it was also called "sweat labor," because the laborers often worked in hot, stuffy rooms for long hours. In some tenements, an entire apartment was turned into a "sweatshop," with as many as ten workers crowded into a room.

3. With scissors, round off the ends of the fan fold, as shown.

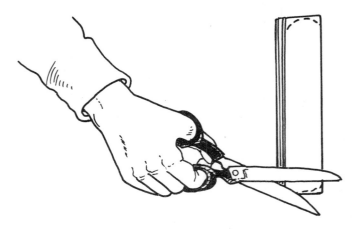

4. Squeeze the center of the fan fold with your fingers and wrap a pipe cleaner around it. Wrap the end of the pipe cleaner around the second pipe cleaner to form a stem.

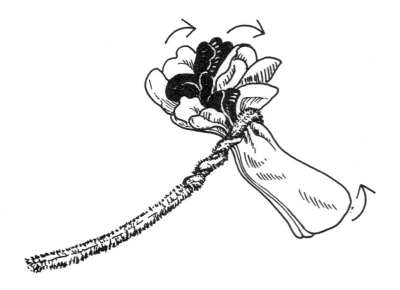

5. Lift the edges of each layer of paper and work them toward the center, arranging them into a blossom shape. Now that you've seen how easy it is, make some more paper flowers in different colors.

 **PROJECT** **BISCUITS WITH FILLING**

Poor people in Europe and America usually could not afford to eat meat every day. To stretch the meat supply, they often used small amounts of it to stuff vegetables, rolls, or pastry. That way, everyone had enough to eat and enjoyed at least a little meat. The recipe you'll follow was used by many immigrant families in the 1890s and was printed in the first *Boston Cooking School Cookbook* in 1896. For the filling, you can use chopped ham, cooked hamburger, or sausage meat. To make a sweet version, you can use jam, marmalade, or maple sugar.

INGREDIENTS
2 cups all-purpose flour
1 teaspoon salt
2½ teaspoons double-acting baking powder
4–6 tablespoons soft butter (room temperature)
¾ cup milk
1 cup well-cooked sausage meat or hamburger, or
  chopped ham

EQUIPMENT
flour sifter
medium-size mixing bowl
mixing spoon
pastry cloth or clean counter top

rolling pin
biscuit cutter, or juice glass, about 2 inches in
  diameter
table knife and fork
cookie sheet
adult helper

MAKES
about 12 filled biscuits (3 to 4 servings)

1. Preheat the oven to 450 degrees F.

2. Measure 1¾ cups of the flour into the sifter and sift it into the mixing bowl.

3. Add the salt and baking powder to the flour. Stir well with the mixing spoon to blend the ingredients.

4. Add 3 tablespoons butter by cutting off small pieces with the table knife and working it into the flour mixture with your fingers. Continue working the butter into the flour until the mixture becomes grainy, like uncooked cream of wheat.

5. With your hand or a spoon, press a hole in the middle of the flour mixture. Pour in the milk all at once.

6. Stir the milk into the dough. Keep stirring for about one minute, until the dough no longer sticks to the sides of the bowl.

7. Sprinkle a little of the remaining flour onto the pastry cloth or counter top, and turn the dough onto it.

8. Knead the dough gently with your hands by folding it over on itself several times until it is smooth. Don't knead it more than a minute or two or the dough will become tough.

9. Rub a little flour on the rolling pin and roll out the dough to a thickness of about ½ inch.

10. Dip the biscuit cutter or glass into the flour on the pastry cloth and cut out the biscuit rounds. Try not to twist the glass or cutter as you press down or the dough will stick to it.

11. Form the leftover dough into a ball, roll it out, and cut more rounds.

12. Spread half of the rounds with a thin coat of butter and a heaping tablespoon of the cooked meat. Place the remaining rounds on top and press them lightly in place.

13. Prick each biscuit with the fork. Place the biscuits close together on the ungreased cookie sheet.

14. Bake for about 12 minutes, or until the biscuits are lightly browned. Ask your adult helper to use the oven mitts to remove the biscuits from the oven. Serve warm.

 # CINNAMON BREAD STICKS

Although canned foods had been widely used in America since the 1860s, many immigrant families had never seen such products until they came to this country. They particularly liked the American invention of condensed milk because the little cans kept the milk fresh in an age when refrigerators had not yet been invented and few poor families could afford an icebox. They used the condensed milk to make whole milk by adding water, and often used it for cooking and baking. This recipe makes an inexpensive dessert that families with little money might have made with condensed milk and a few other ingredients.

INGREDIENTS
1 tablespoon soft butter (room temperature) or
*   cooking oil*
1 12-ounce can condensed milk
2 teaspoons cinnamon
1 teaspoon vanilla
dash of salt
2 slices white bread

EQUIPMENT
piece of wax paper
cookie sheet
medium-size mixing bowl
mixing spoon

The Ice Age: Keeping Food Cool

Modern refrigerators with electric motors were first developed in 1916, but they were too expensive for most families until improvements made them cheaper in the 1930s. From the 1830s to the 1930s, the best way to keep food cool was in an ice chest, or ice box—a large chest that held a big block of ice as well as the food. As the ice melted, the water dripped into a pan underneath the chest. A common scene on every street in the nation was the ice man and his horse-drawn wagon, making regular deliveries of fresh ice to his customers. The ice was "harvested" from ponds and lakes during the winter and stored in ice houses for year-around use.

table knife
spatula
oven mitts
wire cake rack
adult helper

MAKES
2 to 3 dessert or snack servings

1. Preheat the oven to 400 degrees F.

2. Use a piece of wax paper to grease the cookie sheet with butter or cooking oil.

3. Pour the condensed milk into the mixing bowl. Add the cinnamon, vanilla, and salt. Stir the mixture well with the mixing spoon.

4. Cut the bread into pieces, about ¾-inch wide, with the table knife.

5. Dip each bread piece into the cinnamon mixture and place it on the cookie sheet.

6. Bake for 5 to 10 minutes. Check the bread sticks often, since some varieties of bread will brown much faster than others. When the bread sticks are brown, ask your adult helper to use the oven mitts to remove the cinnamon bread sticks from the oven, turn them over with the spatula, then return the cookie sheet to the oven.

7. When the cinnamon bread sticks have browned on the other side, ask your adult helper to remove them from the oven. Use the spatula to place them on a wire rack to cool. Serve warm or at room temperature.

EASTER FUN

Since the Kadinskys did not have to work on Sundays, they turned the day into what Papa called "an adventure." Sometimes they took a picnic to the banks of the Hudson River to watch the sailboats, or to Central Park, where people rode new contraptions called bicycles.

On Easter Sunday, after church, they walked to Fifth Avenue to watch wealthy families in their best outfits ride their carriages up and down the avenue. Mary enjoyed seeing the women's fashions and their elegant hats, while Carl liked the sleek horses and handsome carriages.

Late in the afternoon, Mary and Carl played a game of Polish checkers, then Mama helped them decorate Easter eggs. She showed them how to use a pen and melted wax to draw a design on each egg, then colored the eggs in a dye she had made from onion skins. The eggs turned pale yellow, but the waxed parts remained white. They removed the wax and made a second design, then a third, coloring parts of the eggs tan with a dye made from tea leaves, and other parts red with a berry dye. In the evening, Mary and Carl put on a puppet show, using an oil lamp to light the shadow puppets they had made the previous Sunday.

SHADOW PUPPET

Puppet plays were a favorite form of inexpensive entertainment in the 1890s. Families with little money could pay a few pennies to watch street performers act out plays like one called the *Punch and Judy Show*. Even recent immigrants who knew little English could laugh at whatever trouble Punch got into, and then cheer when his wife Judy or their dog Toby rescued him. Many people made their own puppets—usually shadow puppets, because they were much easier to make and work with than string puppets. They also made their own puppet theaters out of cardboard and decorated them with pictures cut from magazines. Try making two or three puppets with a friend and invent your own show.

MATERIALS

white poster board, 8-by-10 inches
pencil
ruler
scissors
crayons or colored pencils
hole punch
4 small brass paper fasteners (½ inch)

3 thin sticks, 10 to 12 inches long, such as dowels, chopsticks, or bamboo garden stakes
white glue
transparent tape
cardboard box, at least 16-by-32 inches on the largest side (ask your supermarket to save one for you; it's okay if the box has no top.)
craft knife or box cutter (to be used by an adult)
12-by-24-inch sheet of thin white paper, such as wrapping paper or tissue paper
desk lamp or powerful flashlight
table and stool, or two tables
adult helper

1. Draw a puppet character, about 9 inches high, on the poster board. Either copy the drawing shown here, or invent your own puppet character. Notice that the head, body, and legs are one piece, and the four arm pieces are separate. Cut out the five pieces with scissors.

2. Use crayons or colored pencils to color your puppet. The colors won't show on a screen, but the coloring will add a nice touch.

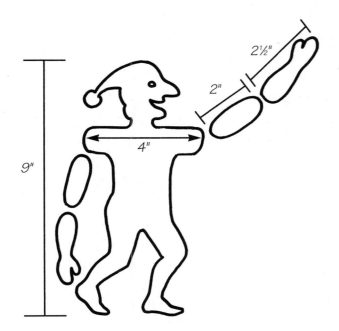

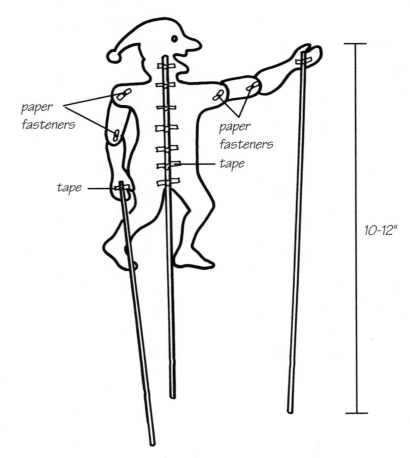

3. Place two arm pieces together so that they overlap at the elbow. Use a hole punch to make a hole through both pieces. Push a paper fastener through both holes and bend back the prongs. Keep the fastener just loose enough so that you can move the arm.

4. Repeat step 3 for the other arm.

5. Position the arms on the puppet's shoulders. Punch holes through both layers and attach the arms with paper fasteners.

6. Run a thin line of glue down the center of the puppet's body. Place one of the sticks on the glue line and press it in place.

7. Squeeze a little glue on each of the puppet's hands. Position the end of a stick on each hand and press it in place. Allow the glued pieces to dry for 5 to 10 minutes.

8. When the glue has dried, you can strengthen the hold by placing pieces of tape across the sticks as shown in the picture.

9. Practice working the puppet by holding the middle stick with one hand and using your other hand to move the arms.

10. To make a puppet theater, you'll use three sides of a cardboard box. Ask your adult helper to use the craft knife or box cutter to remove the bottom of the box, one of the sides, and any top flaps.

11. In the middle side of the box, have the adult cut an opening measuring about 10 inches by 20 inches. Stretch the sheet of thin white paper across the opening and tape it in place as shown in the drawing. This forms the screen for viewing the puppet in silhouette.

12. Place a table and a tall stool (or any other suitable pieces of furniture) close to each other. Place your puppet theater on the edge of the table and the flashlight or desk lamp on the stool. Position the light so that the beam will cast the puppet's shadow onto the screen, as shown. You may have to adjust the position of the light so that the puppet's shadow is the right size on the screen.

13. The puppeteer can sit or kneel on the floor behind the table and operate the puppet from underneath, as shown. The audience sits on the other side of the table and views the action on the screen. When you have everything ready, darken the room, switch on the lamp or flashlight, and start your performance.

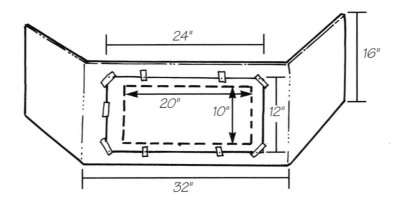

PROJECT DECORATED EASTER EGGS

Colored eggs have been used to celebrate spring in many countries since ancient times and, of course, they are also symbols of Easter. Craftspeople in Poland, Russia, and the Ukraine turned decorated eggs into a delicate and beautiful art. In the 1890s, a Russian named Peter Carl Fabergé became famous for the exquisite porcelain Easter eggs he created for members of Europe's royal families. Fabergé's eggs were decorated with fine gold thread and gems. Other craftspeople tried to imitate the delicate designs, using less costly materials.

Traditional decorated eggs are made with a wax-resist technique, using melted beeswax to resist, or block out, the dye. In this project, you'll use wax crayons in much the same way.

MATERIALS
several sheets of newspaper
apron or smock
small mixing bowl
6 fresh eggs, at room temperature
straight pin
tap water
paper towels
pencil
white crayon
Easter egg dye or food coloring, any colors
3 or 4 paper cups, 9-ounce size or larger
spoon or stick for stirring
bowl or small basket
adult helper

1. Spread several sheets of newspaper on your work surface and place the mixing bowl on it. You'll be working with washable colors, but it's a good idea to wear an apron or smock.

2. Wash the eggs and pat them dry with a paper towel.

3. To blow out the contents of an egg, ask your adult helper to help you poke a pin hole in the top, or pointed end, of the egg. Wiggle the pin back and forth a little to enlarge the hole and to break through the egg membrane.

4. Make a slightly larger hole in the other end of the egg, chipping away a little of the shell with the tip of the pin.

5. Hold the egg just above the bowl with the large hole down. Blow gently through the small hole, pushing the egg contents into the bowl. Save the eggs in the refrigerator for another recipe.

small hole in top

large hole
(about ¼")

Note: Raw eggs have to be handled carefully as a health precaution. Always wash your hands after handling raw eggs. The Cornell University Agricultural Extension Service reports that blowing out the contents of eggs presents little or no risk. However, if there is any concern in your family about this, you can use hardboiled eggs for this project. Many craftspeople use whole, uncooked eggs because the contents will dry up in time, but the risk of breaking makes this a less satisfactory method.

6. Turn on the cold water faucet and run a gentle stream of water through the eggshell. Set the eggshell on a paper towel to dry for 15 to 20 minutes.

7. Repeat steps 3 through 6 with the other eggs.

8. Plan a design for each egg. Remember that you're using a wax-resist method, so the part you draw with the crayon will remain white. For designs, you can try stripes, squiggly lines, dots, stars, or anything else you think of. Draw the design on the egg very lightly in pencil, then go over it with the crayon.

9. Place egg dye or food coloring in paper cups. Add tap water according to the directions on the egg-dye package. If you use food coloring, experiment with a few drops in ¾ cup of water.

10. Put an egg on which you've drawn a crayon design into a cup of dyed water. Use a spoon or stick to roll it around in the dye. Since the egg is very light, you may have to hold it down as you turn it. The longer you keep the egg in the dye, the deeper the color will be.

11. Carefully lift the egg out of the cup. Let any dye in the egg drip back into the cup. Place the egg on a paper towel to dry.

12. Repeat steps 10 and 11 with the other eggs.

13. When the eggs have dried, you can use the crayon to block off other areas of each egg to add a second color, if you wish, and even a third. Display your decorated eggs in a small basket or bowl.

Easter Customs

A number of our modern Easter traditions began in the late 1800s. Americans had colored Easter eggs since colonial times, but German immigrants added something new. They brought the German tradition that colored eggs were hidden in baskets by the Easter hare, or rabbit. By 1880, the custom of the Easter bunny had spread throughout the United States.

The custom of wealthy New Yorkers riding their carriages up and down Fifth Avenue also began about 1880. As this procession became more and more popular in the 1890s, people began calling it the Easter Parade, and the elaborate hats worn by women became known as Easter bonnets.

PROJECT POLISH CHECKERS

The familiar game of checkers, or draughts (pronounced drafts), was developed in Europe nearly a thousand years ago. Over the years, people created different forms of the game. One of the most exciting versions, called Polish checkers, was invented in the 1700s. Polish checkers became so popular in Europe and America in the late 1800s that some experts wrote books of strategy.

Polish checkers is like regular checkers in many ways. The goal of the game is the same—to jump all of the other player's game pieces or to block the pieces so the opponent cannot make a move. But the Polish version is different in two important ways: First, while regular checkers is played on a board with sixty-four squares and each player has twelve game pieces, the board for Polish checkers has a hundred squares, and each player has twenty game pieces, or checkers. The second difference is that the kings in Polish checkers have more power, so strategy in planning moves can be very important.

MATERIALS
several sheets of newspaper
1 piece of white poster board, 10-by-14 inches
1 piece of cardboard, 10 inches square
ruler
pencil
marking pens or crayons, red and black
1 quarter (25-cent piece)
scissors
2 players

1. Spread several sheets of newspaper on your work surface. Place the poster board on it.

2. With ruler and pencil, mark a line across both short ends of the board, 2 inches in from the end. Measure carefully so that the lines are exactly 2 inches from the end all the way across. This 2-inch space at either end is called the tray, where you put your opponent's checkers after you capture them.

3. The center part of your board now forms a perfect 10-inch square. Use pencil and ruler to mark lines exactly 1 inch apart along all four sides as shown.

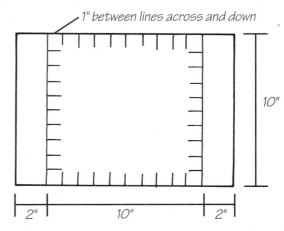

1" between lines across and down

10"

2"   10"   2"

4. With ruler and pencil, carefully connect the lines. Your game board will now have 100 perfect squares.

5. Use the black marking pen or crayon to color in every other square, as shown in the drawing. You can leave the other squares white or color them red.

6. Place the sheet of cardboard on your work surface. Use the quarter as a pattern to draw 40 circles in pencil on the cardboard. Carefully cut out the circles with scissors.

7. With marking pen or crayon, color 20 pieces black on both sides and color the other 20 pieces red. You're now ready to play Polish checkers.

Rules for Polish Checkers

Note: The rules are the same as for regular checkers, except for rule number 7.

1. Each player has 20 checkers. The player with the black checkers always makes the first move, so use any method you wish to choose who has the black.

2. The game is played only on the black squares. Each player places his or her 20 checkers on the black squares closest to the tray.

3. Each player can move only 1 checker per turn, one square at a time, and only on the diagonal to another black square. If the opponent's checker is in the way, the first player jumps that checker, as long as the space being jumped to is free. When a player jumps the opponent's checker, she captures it and places it in her tray.

4. Checkers can only move forward, except when making a jump. Jumps can be made forward or backward. A player can capture more than one piece at a time, as long as each jump is made to an empty square.

5. Once a player touches a checker, he must make a move or lose his turn.

6. When a player's checker is moved to the opponent's last row (the row closest to the opponent's tray), that checker is crowned and becomes a king. (A king is crowned by placing another checker of the same color on top of it.)

7. As in regular checkers, a king can move forward or backward. In Polish checkers, kings have the extra advantage of being able to move diagonally across as many empty spaces as the player wishes, even after making a jump. For example, a king can capture the opponent's checker and then land 3 or 4 spaces beyond in order to be safe from capture, as shown in the illustration.

8. A king can be captured by another king or by a single checker.

9. The game ends when one player has lost all of his or her checkers, or is trapped and cannot make a move. If neither player can make a move, the game ends in a tie, or draw.

player

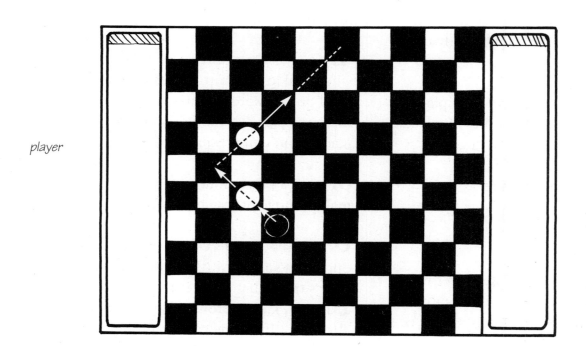

player

STARTING SCHOOL

In April, the Kadinskys learned that Mary and Carl could start school without waiting for the fall term. Papa wore his best clothes to take them to the evening registration and proudly signed the forms. He also registered for himself and Mama to take evening classes in English and citizenship. He reminded the children that free education was one of the greatest gifts America offered.

Mary felt a little uneasy on the first day of school when she saw the large classroom crowded with more than forty other children. But she quickly became more comfortable when she discovered that many of the students were also immigrants who could speak little or no English, including several from Poland. Before long, she was so thrilled to be learning English, she almost forgot she was a newcomer.

The school was called an industrial school, where children could learn work skills, as well as such subjects as reading, penmanship, and math. In her sewing class, where Mary learned to embroider things like tablecloths and petticoats, she embroidered a bookmark for their family Bible. She also stitched a little cloth bag with a drawstring that she planned to give Mama for her birthday in June.

PROJECT DRAWSTRING TRINKET BAG

The invention of the sewing machine in the 1850s took much of the drudgery out of sewing chores. Women no longer had to sew all of a family's clothing by hand. Even people with very little money could now buy inexpensive factory-made clothes. But mending that clothing, or replacing lost buttons still required handiness with a needle and thread. In addition, many women and some men used sewing in creative ways, developing their artistry in embroidery, quilting, and other forms of needlework, or just adding a bit of lace to a machine-made dress.

Girls and young women in Victorian days also used their sewing skills to make practical items, like this trinket bag, which can hold small objects like a comb or hair brush, coins, keys, or some special treasure. If you enjoy working on your drawstring trinket bag, you might want to make more to give as gifts. You can buy inexpensive fabric remnants wherever fabric is sold.

MATERIALS

cotton print fabric, about 10-by-14 inches (small
  prints will work best)
ruler
pencil
scissors
16 to 20 straight pins
sewing needle
thread, in color to match fabric
iron (optional)
ironing board (optional)
⅛-inch or ¼-inch cord, white, gold, or silver, about
  20 inches long (available wherever sewing notions
  are sold)
safety pin
adult helper (for ironing)

1. Place the fabric on your work surface and fold it in half, with the right sides (print sides) facing each other.

2. With ruler and pencil, draw a rectangle on the fabric measuring 8 inches by 6 inches. Make a pencil mark at the halfway point on the two sides and bottom of the rectangle, as shown in the diagram.

3. Draw a curved line connecting the side pencil marks with the bottom pencil mark, as shown, creating a shape that looks like a shirt pocket. Pin the fabric together with straight pins just inside your pencil lines.

4. Cut along the lines with scissors all the way around, giving you two pocket-shaped pieces.

5. Cut a piece of thread about 18 inches long and thread the needle. Run about 6 inches of thread through the eye of the needle, then tie a double knot at the end of the other (longer) strand of thread.

6. Sew the two curved sides together, using a running stitch about ¼ inch in from the edge. To sew running stitches, push the needle up through both layers at A, then down at B, as shown. Come up at C, down at D, and up again at E, and so on.

7. When you reach the top edge of the bag, tie a double knot close to your last stitch, and cut off the extra thread.

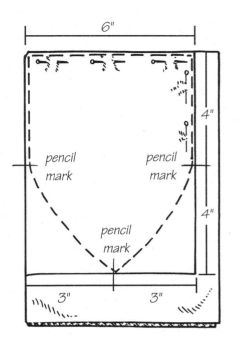

6"
4"
4"
pencil mark   pencil mark
pencil mark
3"   3"

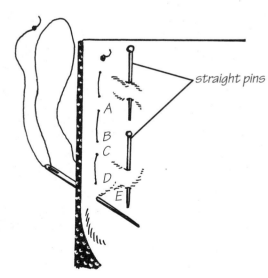

straight pins
A
B
C
D
E

"I Pledge Allegiance . . ."

In 1892, the New York City schools introduced a pledge of allegiance to the flag. The purpose of the pledge was to help immigrants feel that America was their country. At the start of each school session, the students stood facing the flag and recited the line, "I pledge allegiance to my flag and to the republic for which it stands, one nation, indivisible, with liberty and justice for all." About 1940, the wording of the pledge was changed to "the flag of the United States of America" and "one nation, under God, with liberty and justice for all." The students considered it an honor to be the one chosen to hold the flag during the pledge.

8. When you've finished sewing the two sides together, remove the pins. Fold down the top edge of the bag 1½ inches and pin it. This will form the casing for the cord. *Note: You may find it easier to sew the casing if you ask an adult to help you iron the fold before you pin it.*

9. Fit one hand into the opening at the top of the bag to hold it open and sew a running stitch around the casing about ¼ inch from the edge. Tie a double knot close to your last stitch and cut off the extra thread.

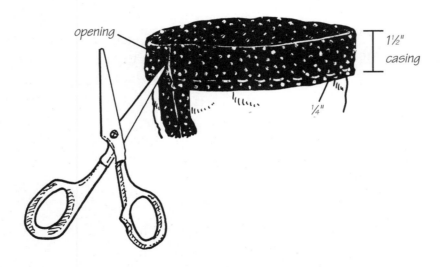

opening

1½" casing

¼"

10. Turn the bag right side out. To make an opening for the cord, carefully cut a stitch or two along the side seams of the casing, as shown.

11. Tie one end of the cord to a closed safety pin. Push the pin into the opening and work it all the way around the casing. Pull the pin out of the opening you started from and untie the cord from the pin.

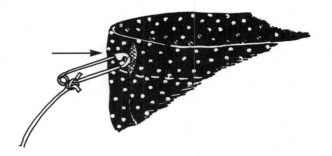

12. Tie a knot about 1 inch from each end of the cord. Pull the ends of the cord to close the bag and tie a single knot or a bow.

PROJECT EMBROIDERED BOOKMARK

Well-to-do Victorian women did not have to make or mend clothing or other things, but most considered sewing a favorite hobby, especially embroidery—decorating fabric with stitched designs. They embroidered all sorts of fabric items, including tablecloths and napkins, sheets and pillow cases, aprons, handkerchiefs, dresses, and scarves. Some also embroidered beautiful pictures, often of flowers, to be framed and hung on walls like paintings. You can experiment with embroidery stitching in this bookmark project, and then try something larger, like a pillow or a T-shirt. Instead of trying to finish the project quickly, take your time and work on your embroidery whenever you have a few spare minutes. That's the way Victorian kids did it.

MATERIALS

sheet of drawing paper
ruler
pencil
8 inches of grosgrain ribbon, 2¼ inches wide, any
   color (available wherever sewing notions are sold)
fabric pen with disappearing ink (optional)
embroidery floss, yellow, white, and green, or any
   3 or 4 colors
scissors
sewing needle

1. On a sheet of paper, use ruler and pencil to draw a rectangle the size of your bookmark: 8 inches by 2¼ inches.

2. Sketch your name and a design on the rectangle. Either use the flower design shown on the next page, or create your own, but keep the design simple for easier stitching. Follow the colors listed in the picture, or choose your own.

3. Copy the letters and design on the grosgrain ribbon. You can either draw lightly in pencil or use a fabric pen with disappearing ink. The advantage of the pen is that mistakes are easy to correct—you simply wait for the ink to disappear, then try again.

4. Choose a color for your name and cut a piece of embroidery floss about 18 inches long in that color. You will see that the floss is made of six strands. Separate three strands for embroidering your name. Thread the needle with the three strands, pushing 5 or 6 inches through the needle eye, then tying a double knot close to the other end.

5. Use a running stitch to embroider your name. To make running stitches, see the drawing for the drawstring trinket bag project. Sew the stitches close together to avoid gaps. When you need more thread, tie a knot close to your last stitch and cut off the small amount of extra thread.

6. Embroider the stem of the flower with a running stitch, using 3 strands of green floss.

7. To make the leaves and the flower petals, you'll use all 6 strands of the floss for a stitch called the lazy daisy. To sew lazy-daisy stitches, come up at A, make a loop the size of the petal or leaf, hold the loop to the ribbon with a finger, and go back down again right next to A. To anchor the loop into the shape of a leaf or petal, come up at B and down at C, then up at D to start another loop.

8. For the center of the flower, sew several short stitches close together, filling in the entire space.

9. If you wish, you can fill in the flower petals and leaves by making long stitches side by side. Place the stitches close enough to each other that little or no ribbon shows through. This is called satin stitching.

10. Cut a notch in one end of the bookmark as shown. Your embroidered bookmark is ready to use.

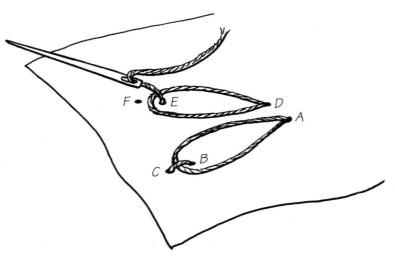

CHAPTER TWO

SUMMER

Summer brought stifling heat to the Kadinskys' crowded tenement neighborhood. There were no air conditioners or electric fans in 1893, so even sitting still to make paper flowers was uncomfortable. On the warmest nights, the Kadinskys put their mattresses on the fire escape, while other families tried to sleep on the rooftops and even on the front steps of the tenements.

In spite of the heat waves, there was plenty of summer fun. Mary and Carl joined other children in street games like marbles, hopscotch, rolling hoops, and a form of baseball called stickball. They often followed one of the icemen until he finally gave them chunks of ice to play with. When the family had a little extra money, Papa took them to an ice cream parlor for ice cream sodas. Their Sunday outings included a colorful circus parade and a trip to the zoo in Central Park.

CONEY ISLAND ADVENTURE

In the spring, Papa Kadinsky had joined an immigrant organization, or club, called the Polish Falcons. By working together, the Falcons were able to help members with matters like finding a better job or a place to live. They also organized regular Sunday outings. Early in July, the Kadinskys joined an excursion to a beach resort called Coney Island. With nearly two hundred club members, they made the two-hour trip in a gaily-decorated steamboat, while a band played popular Polish and American tunes.

Coney Island was packed with people and activities. While wealthy people enjoyed the luxury hotels, restaurants, and a race track, poor people like the Kadinskys and their friends found plenty to do that cost little or nothing. Papa and Carl joined a group of Falcons digging clams for the afternoon picnic. Mary, Mama, and Rose went with others to explore the beach. They watched people riding rented donkeys, waded in the chilly water, and collected seashells. Mary saved the prettiest shells to make a seashell display case.

Every family brought baskets filled with food to eat with the steamed clams and clam broth. Mama had made dozens of sugar-coated walnut dumplings and later showed the children how to use the walnut shells she had saved to make tiny sailboats. She had also helped Mary make stuffed eggs, which, they learned, were called deviled eggs in America. The exciting day ended with a huge fireworks display and a sleepy boat trip home.

PROJECT DEVILED EGGS

Stuffed hard-cooked eggs had been popular in America since colonial days. Then, in the 1800s, people began adding a touch of hot spices to the yolks, and the name was gradually changed from stuffed eggs to deviled eggs. (To "devil" food means to add ingredients that make the dish hot or spicy.)

INGREDIENTS

6 eggs
tap water
3 tablespoons softened butter (room temperature)
2 tablespoons mayonnaise
1 teaspoon cayenne pepper
½ teaspoon dry mustard
dash of salt and pepper

EQUIPMENT

large saucepan
mixing spoon
sharp knife (to be used by an adult)
small mixing bowl
fork
serving dish
adult helper

MAKES

4 to 6 servings

1. Place the eggs in the saucepan. Add enough tap water to cover the eggs. ***Note:*** *Always wash your hands after handling raw eggs.*

2. Turn on the burner to medium heat and bring the water to a boil. When the water starts to boil, reduce the heat a little so that the water simmers rather than boils. Simmer for 15 minutes.

3. As soon as the 15 minutes are up, ask your adult helper to pour off the hot water and run cold water into the saucepan. Crack each egg by tapping it with the mixing spoon to speed the cooling.

4. When the eggs have cooled, peel off the shells and have your adult helper use the sharp knife to cut the eggs in half length-wise.

5. Spoon the yolks into the mixing bowl and mash them with a fork. Add the softened butter, mayonnaise, cayenne pepper, mustard, and a dash of salt and pepper. Mix well with a fork to blend the ingredients into a smooth paste.

6. Place the egg whites on a serving dish and spoon the yolk mixture into them. Serve your deviled eggs at room temperature.

Coney Island

Americans had little interest in beach vacations before the late 1800s. New York's Coney Island, which was first developed about 1860, was one of the nation's earliest beach resorts. The resort grew rapidly and, by the early 1890s, excursion boats and seven railroads carried thousands of vacationers to Coney Island every week. In addition to the beaches, where people "bathed" fully clothed, the resort offered luxury hotels, inexpensive boarding houses, horse races, fireworks, and an amusement park. The idea of an amusement park with rides and other attractions was brand new in 1893. Daring visitors could ride the world's first roller coaster for a nickel, but the Ferris wheel, which was introduced in Chicago that year, was not yet available at Coney Island.

PROJECT SEASHELL DISPLAY CASE

Americans in Victorian days loved to explore nature and display collections of things they had found. They dried and pressed flowers, labeled different stones and rocks, and often displayed stuffed birds and animals. Perhaps the most popular objects to collect were seashells. Some people used their shells to decorate lamps, picture frames, mirrors, and boxes, while others preferred to display the shells in shallow cases with glass covers. They often labeled each specimen with its common name, scientific name, and the location in which it was found.

For your seashell display case, you can buy inexpensive shells at any craft or hobby store, or collect your own at a beach. If you collect shells, make sure there are no living creatures inside (little hermit crabs frequently crawl into shells after the original tenant has departed). You can add variety to your collection by including bits of driftwood, pebbles, or beach glass (pieces of glass that have been worn smooth by wind, waves, and sand).

MATERIALS

several sheets of newspaper
shallow gift box with lid, about 8-by-10 inches, with sides 1½ to 3 inches high (available at discount department stores, often free)
ruler
pencil
scissors
poster paint or acrylic paint—light blue, light green, or sand colored
paint brush
white glue
12 or more shells
driftwood, pebbles, beach glass, optional

for cleaning shells: ½ cup household bleach
2-quart plastic container or pail
tap water
paper towels
¼–½ cup mineral oil (available at drugstores and
supermarkets)
clean rag
adult helper (for handling bleach)

1. Spread several sheets of newspaper on your work surface. Place the box and lid on it. The box itself will be the display case and you'll use the lid to make dividers.

2. To make a divider to run down the center of the box, you'll need a piece of cardboard 10 inches long, plus about 1½ inches on each end for tabs to glue the divider to the sides of the box. The sides of the lid are handy for this. With ruler and pencil, mark 1½ inches around the corner of the lid on the short sides, as shown in the drawing. Cut out the divider and its tabs with scissors.

3. Position the divider in the box, but don't glue the tabs yet. Measure for two or three smaller dividers plus tabs to go from the center divider to the sides of the box, as shown. Mark these with ruler and pencil on the box lid and cut them out with scissors.

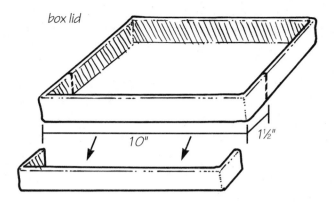

box lid

10"   1½"

4. Use poster paint or acrylic paint to paint the inside of the box. Paint both sides of the dividers and the tabs as well, using the same color. Allow the paint to dry for 15 to 20 minutes.

5. Position the dividers in the box. Spread white glue on each set of tabs and press the tabs against the sides of the box to fix them in place. Let the glue dry for 10 to 15 minutes. Your display case is now ready to use.

6. If you collected your own shells, it's a good idea to clean them before you use them. Ask an adult to help you make a solution of about ½ cup of household bleach and 1 quart of lukewarm water in a plastic container or pail. Swish the shells around in the solution for a few minutes, then rinse them with tap water and place them on paper towels to dry. Rinse your hands well to remove any bleach.

Shell Art at Sea

Interest in collecting and displaying seashells began in Victorian England and spread throughout Europe and the United States. Even sailors at sea took part in the fad. Some seamen etched intricate pictures on shells, creating a variation of scrimshaw (etching on pieces of ivory). Others created what became known as "Sailors' Valentines," even though they gave them as gifts at any time of year. These valentines were small boxes with hinged lids. Inside the box, the sailor-artist placed shells in a beautiful arrangement or a scene.

7. To preserve the color of your shells, put a little mineral oil on a clean rag and gently rub each shell with it.

8. Position your shells in the display case, moving them around until you have an arrangement you like. Put a little glue on the bottom of each shell and fix it in place. You can either lay your display case flat, or lean it against something for easier viewing.

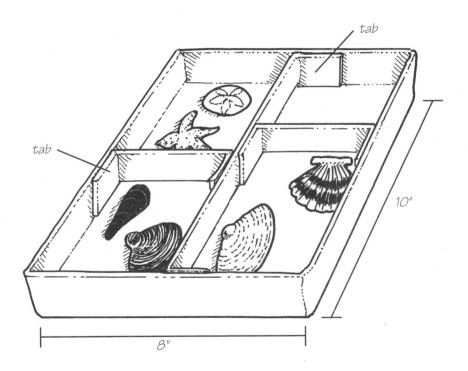

PROJECT WALNUT-SHELL SAILBOATS

Sometime in the 1890s, a group of picnickers in New England discovered the fun of making little sailboats out of walnut shells, and the idea became a favorite at parties and picnics. Any calm body of water, from a pond to a tub, can be used for miniature sailboat races. Make several with friends and experiment with different kinds of sails to see who can make the fastest boat.

MATERIALS

several sheets of newspaper
2 walnuts (for 4 sailboats)
table knife
sheet of white paper (or scraps of different colors of construction paper)
pencil
scissors
crayons, colored pencils, or felt-tip pens, any colors
4 toothpicks
piece of clay (about 1-inch square is enough for 4 sailboats)
white glue
calm body of water (sink, tub, bathtub, swimming pool, or pond)

1. Spread several sheets of newspaper on your work surface, and place the walnuts on them.

2. Open the walnuts by wedging the blade of a table knife between the two halves and gently prying them apart. Save the nut meats—or eat them!

3. For a square sail, cut a piece of paper (white or colored) about 1½ inches wide and 2 inches long. Use another piece the same size, cut on the diagonal, to make two triangular sails.

4. Use crayons, colored pencils, or felt-tip pens to decorate the sails. Add names or numbers, if you wish, especially for racing.

5. Press a small chunk of clay into the bottom of each walnut shell. If necessary, you can add a dab of glue to the clay so it will stick to the shell.

6. Attach each square sail to a toothpick by pushing the toothpick through the sail near the top and bottom, as shown in the drawing on the next page. Bend the sail a little in the middle to help catch the breeze when you blow on it. Press the bottom of the toothpick into the clay.

7. For a triangular sail, glue the long side of the sail to a toothpick, as shown, let the glue dry, and then push the toothpick into the clay. Try adding a small triangular sail to the same toothpick at an angle to the first sail. This will help catch the breeze.

8. Your miniature sailboats are now ready to sail. Place them in the water and blow on them gently to start them moving. Try making sails in different sizes and shapes, or add a second mast and even a third, to see how swift and seaworthy a boat you can make.

MARY'S FLOWER BUSINESS

With help from Mama and the Polish Falcons, Mary found a way to make some money by drying flowers. One of the club members, Mrs. Zieglitz, made her living by selling flowers from a pushcart. She needed people to supply her with dried flowers that she could arrange in bouquets to sell during the autumn and winter months. Mary asked if she could try it and her parents agreed.

The family used two beach outings to collect bags of sand and other club members contributed sand. Mrs. Zieglitz showed Mary how to bury blossoms in the sand and keep them airtight for two or three weeks. Mary kept at it throughout the summer, picking up fresh blossoms every few weeks and giving the dried ones to Mrs. Zieglitz. At the end of the summer, Mary counted her earnings: two dollars and eleven cents. Mary used twenty cents to treat the family to ice cream sodas. Mrs. Zieglitz let her keep a few blossoms and showed her how to use them to make a pretty bouquet.

Mary noticed that the sand she used included different colors, because it had been collected at different beaches. She remembered seeing bottles containing layers of colored sand at a shop on Coney Island and, with Papa's help, she arranged layers of the colored sand in a bottle to create an attractive display.

 **COLORED-SAND BOTTLE**

Part of the fun of collecting natural objects like shells, stones, and sand in Victorian days was in gathering them from different places. Railroads and steamboats now made it easier and less expensive for people to travel, and many collectors liked to gather items from distant places, including other parts of the world. Travelers to other countries were often asked to bring back stones or a jar of sand for some young collector back home.

For your colored-sand bottle, you can buy sand in different colors at a hobby or craft store. You can also use beach sand you've collected, or plain sand from a building supply store and follow the directions below to make different colors. Your colored-sand bottle will create an interesting and colorful decoration for your room.

MATERIALS
several sheets of newspaper
5 paper cups, 9-ounce size or larger
pail of clean sand, about 1 quart, or colored sand
    from hobby or craft store
tap water
food coloring or powdered fabric dye, any 4 colors
stir stick or plastic spoon
paper towels

bottle or jar with lid, 1 quart or smaller
drinking straw, or piece of wire, 8 to 10 inches long

1. Spread several sheets of newspaper on your work surface and place the paper cups on top.

2. Using one of the cups as a scoop, fill the other 4 cups to the halfway point with sand. Add just enough water to each cup to cover the sand.

3. Use a plastic spoon or stir stick to stir in a few drops of food coloring, or a little fabric dye, using a different color for each cup. Stir thoroughly until the sand in each cup has changed color, adding more dye or coloring if necessary. Allow the sand to soak in the dye for about 10 minutes.

4. Carefully pour off any colored water that hasn't been absorbed, then spread the sand on paper towels to dry, keeping the colors separate.

5. Repeat steps 3 and 4 to make four more half-cups of colored sand. Use the same colors as before, or different ones if you prefer. After this second batch has been spread on paper towels, allow the sand to dry overnight.

6. When the sand is dry, spoon enough of one color of sand into the bottle to make a layer 1 to 2 inches high. Add a layer of the second color, then the third and the fourth. Avoid shaking or tipping the bottle or else the layers will start to mix together. Keep on adding layers of different colors until the sand is about ½ inch from the top of the bottle.

7. Push the wire or straw into the bottle, keeping it as close to the side of the bottle as possible, and push it all the way to the bottom. As you pull the wire out, you'll see the layers run into each other, producing a unique and colorful pattern.

8. Repeat step 7 all the way around the bottle, creating a rainbow of colored sands.

9. Pour more sand into the bottle to fill it to the very top, then tighten the lid. Since the bottle is completely full, the sand will stay in the pattern you created.

Street Vendors

City streets in the 1890s were crowded with vendors selling their wares from sidewalk stalls, pushcarts, or horse-drawn wagons. Items on sale in a single city block might include fruits and vegetables, coal, second-hand clothes, kitchen knives, flowers, pots and pans, and more. Even children could earn a dollar or two a week selling things like newspapers, rags, matches, or flowers, or else by running errands or shining shoes.

PROJECT SAND-DRIED FLOWERS

Dried flowers will keep much of their original color for months and even years. Flowers can be dried by hanging them in a dark, warm place, or by flattening them in a plant press. A third method, sand drying, is particularly good for flowers that have thick blossoms, such as roses, zinnias, or chrysanthemums. Use your dried blossoms to make a year-round display and save some to use in the next project.

MATERIALS

8 to 12 flowers with thick blossoms (roses, mums, carnations, or marigolds will work well)

scissors

several sheets of newspaper

piece of string

2 pails of clean sand

small, sturdy box with lid (a shoe box is perfect), or an old cookie tin

sand shovel or large spoon

toothpick

masking tape

small paint brush

green florist's wire (available in the craft and hobby section of discount department stores)

3 to 4 sprigs of rosemary, baby's breath, lavender, or heather (available at florist shops or department stores at little cost)

paper lace doily, 6 to 8 inches in diameter
18-inch piece of ½-inch ribbon, any color

1. Before you pick flowers from a garden or the wild, make sure you have permission, and take only as much as you need. Try to pick on a sunny day—late in the morning, after the dew has dried. Cut a few inches of stem and some leaves as well. If the blossoms are wet, let them dry in a warm place before you work with them.

2. Spread several sheets of newspaper on your work surface and place the flowers on top.

3. Cut the stems 1½ to 2 inches below each blossom. Tie the leftover stems and leaves in a bunch and hang them in a warm, dark place, like a closet, to dry for a week or two.

4. Fill the bottom of the box with about 2 inches of sand. Place the blossoms in the sand with the stems down, except for flowers that have a radiating (or circle) blossom, like daisies or black-eyed Susans, which can be placed stem-side up.

5. Carefully shovel sand over each blossom and in between the petals. You want to get rid of any air pockets around the blossoms. Use a toothpick to push sand gently around and between the petals.

6. Add enough sand to cover all the blossoms with about 1 inch of sand. Place the lid on the box and seal the edges with masking tape so that the box is airtight. (The tape isn't necessary if you're using a cookie tin.) Store the box in a warm, dry place for 2 weeks.

7. After two weeks, remove the tape and the lid. Gently uncover one blossom to test it. If the petals feel dry, like paper, the flowers are ready; if not, replace the lid and allow an additional few days for drying.

8. When the blossoms are dry, carefully remove them from the sand. Handle them by the stems as much as possible, since the petals will be quite brittle. Use a small paint brush to brush off any leftover sand.

9. Untie the string from the stems and leaves. Use a short piece of florist's wire to attach a stem and a leaf or two to each blossom. Arrange several of the blossoms into a bouquet, surrounding the flowers with a sprig or two of lavender, baby's breath, or other filler.

10. Form the doily into a cone shape with your bouquet inside. Wrap the bottom of the doily around the stems, then tie it firmly with a piece of ribbon 5 or 6 inches long. Tie one end of a 12-inch piece of ribbon to the top of the doily cone by threading the ribbon through a hole in the doily, then tying a knot at the back. Tie the other end to the opposite side of the cone, as shown. Use this ribbon loop to hang the bouquet from a tack in the wall, or from the edge of a mirror or picture.

THE SETTLEMENT HOUSE

Late in the summer, the Kadinskys learned about an organization in their neighborhood called the Henry Street Settlement House. The settlement had been formed by a group of young women from Smith College. Their purpose was to help immigrant families get through the hard times and adjust to life in America. The settlement house workers organized holiday celebrations, parties, plays, and concerts, and they offered classes in many subjects, including English, cooking, music, and crafts.

The Henry Street Settlement House had something for everyone in the Kadinsky family. Papa joined a club of chess and checker players. Carl joined a drama group so that he could act in plays, and Mary took an English class she thought would help her when school started again. There was even a program for Rose called a kindergarten, an idea that was just catching on throughout the country.

Best of all, Mama, instead of taking a class, was asked if she would give one—showing people how to make Polish paper cutouts.

Mary found that the settlement house was a great place to go when she couldn't play outside. She made new friends and learned lots of games, like a new marble game called tic-tac-taw. And she joined Mama's group often to learn more about making Polish paper cutouts.

PROJECT POLISH PAPER CUTOUTS

In the early 1800s, farm families in Poland developed a wonderful art form called *wycinanka ludowa* (vi-chee-NON-kah loo-DOH-vah), which means "folk paper art." The folk artists cut complicated patterns in folded paper, then unfolded the paper to produce a beautiful symmetrical design. These cutouts are particularly striking when placed against a background of a contrasting color, such as a white design on a black or dark blue backing. Polish paper cutouts are still popular today, both as wall hangings and as greeting cards.

The early Polish cutouts were made to celebrate Easter, and the most common symbol was the rooster, heralding the rising of Christ on Easter morning. After about 1850, the cutouts were used throughout the year and artists used many different subjects for their designs, including trees, flowers, stars, and farm scenes. You can make your Polish paper cutout using the traditional rooster pattern shown here, or create your own design.

MATERIALS

sheet of thin white paper, such as typing paper, about 7-by-9 inches
pencil
scissors
manicure scissors (optional)
construction paper or poster board, 8½-by-11 inches, any dark color
sheet of scrap paper
rubber cement

1. Fold the paper in half the long way, and press the crease flat. The fold will form the center of the design, so you will really be drawing only half the picture.

2. Draw your design on the paper, making use of the fold as the center. The design should be all one piece, as shown, and the arrow on the picture shows you where to cut to get at the inner part of the design. You might find it helpful to shade in the parts of the picture you're going to be cutting away.

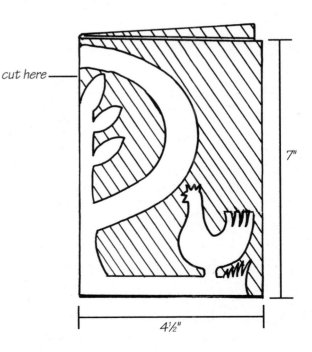

cut here

7"

4½"

Polish Paper Art

One of the most amazing things about Polish paper cutouts is that the folk artists of the 1800s used the same large shears they used for shearing sheep. Somehow, they used these clumsy-looking tools to make designs that are often as intricate as fine lace.

The Polish farm families cut their designs out of colored paper, then pasted them directly on the whitewashed walls of their houses. They sometimes pasted cutouts on the walls of their barns as well, for the cows, horses, and sheep to enjoy.

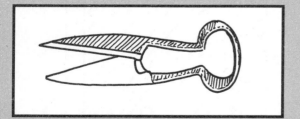

3. Carefully cut out the main design with scissors. You can cut details, like fringes in the rooster's tail, later. If you find it difficult to cut the inner part of the design, try using manicure scissors. Use the sharp point of a pencil to make a hole for the eye.

4. Add scalloping to the tree by cutting small wedges all the way around, as shown in the picture. Handle the design carefully to avoid tearing the paper, although small tears or mistakes can usually be corrected when you glue the design to the dark backing.

5. Open the paper and press the design flat on your work surface, flattening the crease as much as you can.

6. Place the design face down on a sheet of scrap paper and carefully cover the entire back with rubber cement. (Because of the many small edges on the design, rubber cement will be much easier to work with than white glue or craft glue.)

7. Position the design on the center of the dark backing, so that the borders are even all the way around, and press it in place. Press every part of the design so that it sticks to the backing. If any small edges don't stick, carefully add a little more rubber cement.

8. When the rubber cement has dried, carefully rub off any excess cement with your finger. Pin your finished Polish paper cutout on a wall of your room. Now that you know how to make the cutouts, try making smaller ones to use as very special greeting cards.

PROJECT TIC-TAC-TAW

Many different games of marbles were popular throughout the 1800s, and the games became even more popular in the 1890s. Kids found that the games were perfect for city sidewalks and alleys, and there was almost no cost involved. New variations of the basic game were developed, including one called tic-tac-taw. The game is like tic-tac-toe, but players use marbles instead of pencil and paper. The word *taw* refers to a player's special shooting marble; this could be the player's lucky marble or one that is a little larger and heavier than regular marbles. While marbles games are usually played outdoors, tic-tac-taw can be adapted to indoor play.

MATERIALS
10–12 marbles for each player
chalk (for playing on pavement)
5 to 6 feet of string (for playing indoors)
scissors
transparent tape or masking tape (for indoors)
2 players

Shooting marbles
Players must always shoot their marbles in the official way: Place the knuckles of your middle and index finger on the ground and put a marble in the crook of your index finger, as shown on the next page. Use your thumb to flick the marble

along the ground, not through the air or with big bounces. Remember always to keep at least one knuckle on the ground—shooting a marble is also called "knuckling down."

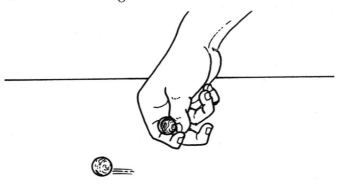

1. On pavement, use chalk to make a grid just like tic-tac-toe, with the lines about 12 inches apart. Indoors, cut four pieces of string, each thirty-six inches long, and tape these in a grid on the floor. (Wood or tile floors work better than carpets.)

2. Mark a shooting line about 6 feet from the grid, using chalk outdoors, taped string indoors. Try shooting some marbles at this distance. Move the shooting line closer to the grid, or farther away, until you have a distance that feels comfortable—so that it isn't too easy to place three marbles in a row, or too difficult either.

3. To see who shoots first, both players pitch one marble toward the center square. The player who comes closest to the square's center shoots first.

4. Each player has one shot per turn. The goal is to place 3 marbles in a row—straight across, up and down, or on the diagonal. A player can also try to knock the opponent's marble off a square, or at least land in the same square. If both players have marbles in the same square, neither can use it to form a row.

5. The first player to place three in a row wins that round. If neither player can form a row, that round ends in a tie, or "cat." Usually, the first player to win 10 rounds wins the game, but players frequently change that rule to have a game consist of fewer rounds or more rounds. You can make this decision before play begins or at any time during the game.

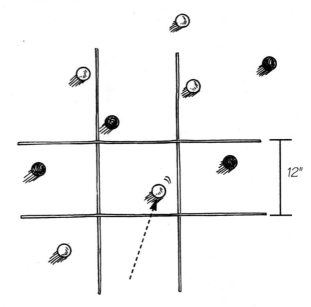

12"

CHAPTER THREE

AUTUMN

On a September evening in 1893, William Hobart had the thrill of riding in the cab of a railroad steam engine as it puffed into New York City's Grand Central Station. The engine was pulling only the three railroad cars that made up the Hobart family's private train. The Hobarts were returning from a month's vacation at their cabin in the Adirondack Mountains.

The family had enjoyed boating, fishing, and hiking in the Adirondacks, but everyone was happy to be home. They had moved into their new house only a few weeks before this trip, so everything still seemed brand new. As their carriage pulled up to the house, they were delighted to see that the servants had turned on the downstairs lights to welcome them home. Of all the new things in their house, the electric lights were still the most exciting.

SCHOOL DAYS

Before breakfast each day, the Hobart family and their servants gathered in the drawing room for morning prayers. Lucy ate breakfast with the family, although young children in most wealthy households ate their meals in the nursery. Lucy's nanny, Margaret, then took her to a private school and William walked with them on the way to his school.

William liked his new school, a private school for boys, partly because he could take a lot of science courses. He also enjoyed sports at the school, including a new game called basketball, which had been invented only two years earlier.

After school, he often headed for his basement workshop. Some days, he pretended he was a great inventor, like Thomas Edison or Alexander Graham Bell. William even tried to rig up tin-can telephones with his friend Alice Wilson, who lived next door.

They carefully stretched the string between their houses, but the distance was too great and they ended up shouting so loudly they didn't need the tin cans and string. Another day, Alice showed William how to make a decoupage box to give to his mother as a present.

PROJECT DECOUPAGE BOX

Many people in Victorian America, adults as well as kids, liked to keep scrapbooks of pictures they had cut from magazines. This activity became so popular that some companies published sheets filled with small pictures called "scraps" for people to cut out.

Another popular use of scraps was for the craft of decoupage—covering a box or other object with small cutout pictures. Decoupage was started in France in the early 1800s, and the name comes from another French word, découper, which means "to cut up." In the 1890s, people used decoupage to decorate boxes, small items of furniture, and even Easter eggs. They then coated the surface with varnish, sometimes applying twenty coats or more. For your decoupage project, two coats of acrylic varnish should be enough. You can collect pictures from old magazines, brochures, or greeting cards, and you can also make colorful designs for small objects from used postage stamps.

MATERIALS

old magazines, greeting cards, brochures, used postage stamps
scissors
several sheets of newspaper
sturdy cardboard box, such as a shoebox or smaller gift box
white glue
small bowl or dish
tap water
craft stick, or other stick for stirring
piece of sponge
acrylic varnish
paintbrush, 1 to 1½ inches wide

1. First, decide on a theme for your box—the kinds of pictures you want to display. Your theme might be horses, baseball, flowers, or any other favorite subject.

2. Collect and cut out plenty of pictures—you'll be covering the entire surface of the sides and lid of your box. Smaller pictures work best because they can be fit together without much overlapping or trimming.

3. Spread several sheets of newspaper on your work surface. Put the box, lid, and your picture collection on top.

4. Before you begin gluing pictures on the box, experiment with different arrangements. You might plan to put a favorite picture in the center of the lid, for example, or to surround a large picture with several small ones.

5. When you have an overall design in mind, pour a little white glue into a small bowl or dish. Add a little tap water to thin the glue, and mix it well with a stir stick. Use a small piece of dampened sponge to spread the thinned glue on the back of each picture. Cover the entire back surface so that no corners or edges turn up.

6. Fit the pictures close together so that as little of the box shows as possible. You can overlap the pictures when necessary for an even closer fit. If any pictures overlap the edges of the lid or the box, trim off the excess with scissors.

7. When all your pictures are in place, allow about 10 minutes for the glue to dry, then use the paintbrush to apply two coats of acrylic varnish. (*Note: Acrylic varnish is not oil-based and it is safe to use; however, we do recommend applying it with a brush, rather than using acrylic spray.*) Allow an hour drying time between coats (check the directions on the bottle for drying time). When the second coat has dried, your first decoupage project is finished. What will you keep in your decoupage box?

PROJECT TIN-CAN TELEPHONE

Alexander Graham Bell invented the telephone in 1876 and by the early 1890s many American families and businesses had installed the device. During these years, kids tried to create their own versions of Bell's great invention. None of the kids' inventions worked very well, of course, but in this project, you and a friend can try the most successful of the imitations.

MATERIALS

2 tin cans (soup cans work well)
sheet of thin, strong paper, such as typing paper, or
    mailing envelopes containing plastic, such as Tyvek
pencil
drawing compass (optional)
scissors
2 strong rubber bands
30 feet of strong thread or thin string, such as kite string
sewing needle
toothpick, or 2 scraps of thin dowel about 1 inch long
mineral oil, available at supermarkets and drug
    stores (optional)

1. Remove the labels and both lids from two clean cans.

2. Place one can on the sheet of paper and trace around it with pencil. Draw a second circle 1 inch larger around the first circle. You can use a drawing compass to make this larger circle or draw it freehand, since the measurement does not have to be exact.

3. Cut out the larger paper circle with scissors. Don't erase the pencil line of the smaller circle. Make a second paper circle the same way. These two circles will be the diaphragms for your telephones. (The diaphragm is a thin disk that vibrates rapidly as it transmits sound waves.)

4. To fit the paper diaphragm over one end of a can, cut slits about 1 inch apart all the way around the outer circle, as shown. Be careful not to cut into the inner circle.

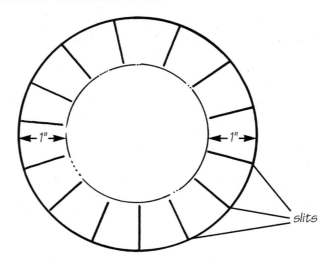

5. Center a diaphragm over the end of one can and fold down the edges. Hold the diaphragm in place with a rubber band. The paper should fit as tightly as possible, like the head of a drum, so that it will vibrate. If necessary, double the rubber band for a tighter fit.

6. Thread one end of the string or thread through the eye of a sewing needle.

7. Push the needle through the center of the paper diaphragm. Reach into the can and pull the needle through. Be careful not to enlarge the hole made by the needle.

8. Remove the string or thread from the needle and tie the end around a piece of dowel or half a toothpick. This will keep the thread from pulling out of the hole when you stretch the line taut.

9. Repeat step 5 with the other can. Thread the needle with the other end of the string or thread and repeat steps 7 and 8. Your telephone is now ready to test.

10. Hold one can while your partner holds the other and walk away from each other until the string between you is taut. Be careful not to pull so hard that you pull the diaphragm off. Make sure the line is straight; if it touches any other object, like a tree limb, the vibrations will be blocked.

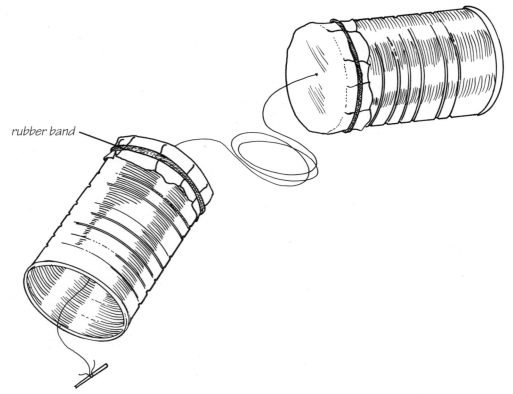

rubber band

11. One person talks directly into the open end of the can, while the listener holds the open end of the other can against his or her ear. If the line is taut, and both diaphragms fit tightly, the sound vibrations will be carried down the line, through the diaphragm, and into the listener's ear. You'll be able to carry on a conversation, taking turns speaking and listening.

12. Kids in Victorian days used oiled paper to make a more effective diaphragm. You can rub some mineral oil on each diaphragm with your fingers to see if that improves the sound.

Mr. Bell's Electrical Toy

When Alexander Graham Bell invented the telephone in 1876, he called it a "speaking telegraph," and he offered to sell it to the Western Union Telegraph Company. But the president of Western Union was not interested. "What use would we have for an electrical toy?" he asked. Other people also had trouble thinking how the telephone would be used. Going to a Western Union office to send a telegram was perfectly convenient. Why would people go to a telegraph office to send a message by telephone?

Gradually people began to see that telephones could be used in people's homes and offices. The first telephone company was formed in New Haven, Connecticut, in 1878. Others soon followed. By 1880, there were more than 50,000 telephones and the number soared after that.

WILDERNESS OUTING

Late in September, Mr. Hobart and another father took William and four other boys on a weekend camping trip. Like many wealthy parents, Mr. Hobart wanted William to experience a little of the rugged outdoor life of America's pioneers. The boys and the two fathers loaded a large coach with supplies and headed out of the city in the predawn darkness. Each of the boys had a chance to drive the two-horse team until they reached a camping site overlooking the Hudson River.

William was already an experienced outdoorsman because of his summers in the Adirondacks, so he could help teach the other boys skills like catching, cleaning, and cooking fish. The campers learned how to gather berries, nuts, and edible mushrooms, and they even managed to start a fire without matches. On nature hikes, the two fathers helped the boys make plaster casts of leaves and of animal footprints, including the prints of a large black bear.

For one evening meal, William and another boy prepared corn oysters and fried brook trout. That same night, a thunderstorm gave Mr. Hobart a chance to demonstrate what lightning is, and the boys tried to measure how close some of the lightning bolts were coming.

 # CREATING AND MEASURING LIGHTNING

Scientists in the 1800s performed thousands of experiments in their efforts to understand electricity. They learned that static electricity is created when negative charges build up in a cloud and leap to positive charges in another part of the cloud or in another cloud. This leap is called a "static discharge," or what most people would call a bolt of lightning. Kids in Victorian days liked to try out some of the more simple techniques for creating a static discharge—a kind of mini-lightning bolt—as you'll be doing in this activity. And, during thunderstorms, they also used a simple formula for measuring how far away a lightning bolt had struck.

1. Creating Lightning

MATERIALS
eraser
sewing needle
balloon
piece of silk or wool, such as a scarf or mitten

1. Place the eraser on your work surface and push the needle into it so that the needle sticks straight up.

2. Inflate the balloon and tie it closed.

3. Darken the room and rub the piece of silk or wool on the balloon several times.

4. Slowly move the balloon closer and closer to the needle. Watch for the spark to leap between the needle and the balloon. By changing the positive and negative charges in the two objects, you created a tiny static discharge.

2. Measuring the Distance of Lightning

When lightning strikes, you see the flash of light instantly because light travels at such a great speed. Sound travels much more slowly, about 1 mile in 5 seconds. By measuring how long it takes the sound of thunder to reach you, you can get a rough idea of how far away the lightning is. Follow this simple formula:

1. When you see a flash of lightning, count the seconds until you hear the thunder.

2. Divide the number of seconds by 5 to arrive at the approximate distance. If you counted 8 seconds, for example, the lightning is about 1.6 miles away (8 divided by 5 = 1.6).

Unlocking the Secrets of Electricity

Joseph Henry, one of America's greatest scientists, performed hundreds of experiments with lightning and electricity. His experiments increased our scientific understanding of electricity and enabled Henry to develop powerful electromagnets, and the first electric motor. He helped to organize the Smithsonian Institution in Washington, D.C., as well as the U.S. Weather Bureau and the National Academy of Science.

Henry was interested in understanding nature, rather than in gaining fame or fortune for himself. In the 1830s, he provided Samuel F. B. Morse with the knowledge Morse needed to invent the telegraph. In the 1870s, when Henry was nearly eighty years old, he helped Alexander Graham Bell work out several electrical problems so that he could complete his invention of the telephone. Joseph Henry had helped create two of the most important advances in human communication—the telegraph and the telephone—but he asked for nothing for himself.

PROJECT PLASTER LEAF CASTS

The Victorians' love of nature and collecting also found expression in making plaster of paris casts of natural objects. While making casts indoors is the easiest way, you can also try casting outdoors if you're in an area where you can find animal footprints in soft ground. Cut the bottom out of an aluminum pie tin and fit the ring formed by the sides over the footprint, then follow the directions below. Indoors or out, you'll have to work fast once you mix the plaster of paris because it sets up (hardens) quickly.

MATERIALS

several sheets of newspaper
4 or more leaves (summer or autumn)
disposable aluminum pie tin
5-pound bag plaster of paris (available in hardware departments or stores)
plastic paint bucket or empty can for mixing
tap water
paint stir stick (free wherever paints are sold) or large spoon
large paper clip
poster paint or acrylic paint, any color
small paintbrush, about ½-inch wide

1. Spread several sheets of newspaper on your work surface.

2. Choose one, two, or three leaves that will fit in the bottom of the pie tin without touching the sides. When you have an arrangement you like, moisten the smooth side of the leaves with a little water and place them in the pie tin smooth side down. (The water will help hold them in place.)

3. Pour enough plaster of paris powder into a paint bucket or can to fill the pie tin. Slowly add tap water, stirring constantly, to create a loose, syrup-like paste. Remember to work quickly!

4. Pour a little plaster of paris directly onto each leaf to fix it in place. Now slowly pour all of the plaster into the pie tin, all the way to the top of the sides if you've mixed that much.

5. While the plaster is still wet, straighten a large paper clip at the bend so that it forms a long S shape. Press the smaller end of the paper clip into the plaster of paris near the top edge. You can then use the upper part of the clip as a hanger when the cast is dry.

6. Allow the plaster of paris to set for about 30 minutes, then carefully remove it from the pie tin. Keep the leaves in place.

7. With poster paint or acrylic, paint around the leaves in any color you choose; the leaves will then stand out white against the darker background. Let the paint dry for 15 to 20 minutes.

8. Carefully peel away each leaf. Use the paper clip as a hanger if you want to hang the casting on a wall of your room.

PROJECT CORN OYSTERS

The tasty fritters in this recipe, which don't really have oysters in them, were called corn oysters because, when cooked, they looked like fried oysters. Victorian Americans usually served corn oysters as a side dish with dinner, but they also served them like pancakes for breakfast, topped with powdered sugar or maple syrup. You can try this easy-to-fix dish either way.

INGREDIENTS

1 egg
1 #2 can whole kernel corn (18 to 20 ounces)
⅓ cup flour
½ teaspoon salt
¼ teaspoon pepper
¼ cup milk
3 to 4 tablespoons butter or cooking oil
maple syrup or confectioner's sugar (for breakfast)

EQUIPMENT

medium-size mixing bowl
fork
colander or large strainer
mixing spoon
large frying pan
spatula
paper towels
serving platter
adult helper

MAKES

3 to 4 servings

1. Crack the egg into the mixing bowl and stir it vigorously with the fork. Remember to wash your hands after handling raw egg.

2. Use the colander or strainer to drain the liquid off the corn. Add the corn to the egg and stir with the mixing spoon.

3. Stir in the flour a little at a time.

4. Add the salt, pepper, and milk. Stir the mixture well to blend all the ingredients.

5. Put 3 tablespoons of butter or cooking oil in a large frying pan and turn the heat to medium high. Use a spatula to spread the oil or butter evenly.

6. With an adult's help, drop 5 or 6 separate spoonfuls of the batter into the hot oil.

7. Cook the corn oysters 2 to 3 minutes, until the underside is lightly browned, then turn them with the spatula and brown the other side.

8. Place several paper towels on a serving platter. Use the spatula to take the cooked corn oysters out of the oil and put them on the paper towels to drain. Cover the corn oysters with more paper towels to keep them warm.

9. Cook and drain the rest of the corn oysters the same way, adding a little more butter or oil to the frying pan if necessary. When you've cooked all the corn oysters, remove the paper towels and serve immediately.

A Famous Outdoorsman

A boy named Teddy was the son of wealthy New York parents who worried about him because he was sick so often. The boy's father encouraged him to build up his strength through vigorous outdoor activity. Teddy grew to love the outdoor life. He often camped in the Adirondack Mountains and, in the 1880s, he moved to the Western frontier where he operated a cattle ranch for several years. He grew up to be a strong, energetic man who continued to urge Americans to enjoy a more rugged outdoor life. His full name was Theodore Roosevelt and, in 1901, he became president of the United States.

A LUNCHEON PARTY

William's new friend and neighbor, Alice Wilson, was planning a luncheon party as part of her twelfth birthday celebration, and she asked William to help her. Arranging the party was actually part of Alice's education, since entertaining guests would be one of her important duties as an adult. Like most girls in well-to-do families, Alice did not go to school. Her parents believed that formal schooling was unnecessary because she would never have to work outside the home. Instead, the Wilsons hired a tutor to help Alice with reading, writing, history, geography, and math. From her mother, Alice learned other useful skills, such as sewing, weaving, and managing the household.

William was happy to help with the party preparations. While Alice arranged dried flowers for a centerpiece on the luncheon table, William wrote out name cards for each of the guests. They planned the menu together, featuring cold roast beef, salad, fruit, a punch to drink— and for dessert a New York cheesecake, which

Alice had recently learned to make. William set up games to play, including a pebble target game he had made. They wrote the party invitations on balloons, then mailed the deflated balloons to Alice's friends.

PROJECT · PARTY INVITATIONS

Wealthy Americans gave very elaborate dinner parties in the 1890s. A hostess often made imaginative invitations for the people on her guest list. The invitations were usually hand delivered by a servant rather than sent through the mail. Most invitations included a polite request that the guest reply, using the initials R.S.V.P. for the French phrase, *Répondez, s'il vous plait* (ray-PON-day SEE voo-PLAY), meaning "please respond" or reply. When you're planning a party, try this creative invitation developed by a young Chicago woman in the 1890s.

MATERIALS
1 balloon for each invitation
felt-tip pen, medium point, any color
1 envelope for each invitation

1. Blow up a balloon to about half its maximum size. You can either hold the end closed with one hand or tie it with a piece of string that can be untied easily.

2. Use the felt-tip pen to write out the invitation on the balloon. You'll find it's helpful to rest the balloon on a table or desk to steady it for writing. And, of course, you don't want to press too hard with the pen!

3. Let the air out of the balloon, place it in an addressed envelope, and continue with the rest of the balloons. Seal the envelopes and mail.

The Changing Role of Women

Most wealthy Americans in the 1890s continued to believe that a woman's place was in the home, raising children and managing the household. Some people even believed that women did not have the ability to study difficult college subjects.

A growing number of women defied these traditional beliefs. In the late 1800s, several women's colleges were established and some universities allowed women to enroll. By 1900, more than 1,000 women had become lawyers, 3,000 were ministers, and 7,500 were doctors. Some daughters of well-to-do families worked for organizations like the settlement houses in order to help the millions of poor people who were struggling to survive. More and more women were also demanding their right to vote in political elections, a right they finally won in 1920.

PROJECT NEW YORK CHEESECAKE

German immigrants brought the original recipe for cheesecake to America in the 1870s. A chef in a New York restaurant changed the recipe in the late 1880s by creating a lighter filling and a crust made with graham crackers. Graham crackers had been invented some years earlier by Dr. Sylvester Graham, and they were considered an excellent health food. To make sure they were getting the healthier graham cracker crust, patrons of restaurants and bakeries began asking for the New York cheesecake.

Over the years, several varieties of New York cheesecake have been developed. In this project, you'll follow one of the easiest recipes and you'll use a ready-made graham cracker pie shell.

INGREDIENTS

3 8-ounce packages of cream cheese
1 cup sugar
4 eggs
3 tablespoons all-purpose flour
4 tablespoons sour cream
1 teaspoon vanilla
1 lemon
1 9-inch graham cracker pie shell

EQUIPMENT

medium-size mixing bowl
mixing spoon
egg beater (optional)
grater
paring knife (to be used by an adult)
oven mitts
wire cooling rack
adult helper

MAKES

6 to 8 servings

1. Before you begin, let the cream cheese stand at room temperature for about 1 hour to soften it. Keep the pie shell in the refrigerator until you're ready to use it.

2. Preheat the oven to 300 degrees F.

3. Place the cream cheese in the mixing bowl and beat it with a mixing spoon until it's smooth.

4. Stir in the sugar, then the eggs, one at a time. Beat the mixture well with the mixing spoon. If you find it's hard to beat the mixture with the spoon, use an egg beater. Remember to wash your hands after handling raw egg.

5. Add the flour, sour cream, and vanilla. Beat with the spoon or egg beater.

6. Use the grater to make 1 teaspoon of lemon rind. Stir this into the mixture.

7. With an adult's help, cut the lemon in half and squeeze 1 teaspoon of lemon juice into the other ingredients. (Save the rest of the lemon for other uses.) Beat the ingredients one more time.

8. Pour the mixture into the chilled pie shell. Use the mixing spoon to spread it evenly.

9. Bake for one hour. Then turn off the heat, open the oven door, and let the cheesecake rest in the warm oven for 15 minutes.

10. Using oven mitts, remove the cheesecake from the oven and place it on the wire rack to cool.

11. When the cake is at room temperature, put it in the refrigerator for an hour or two before serving.

PEBBLE TARGET GAME

In the 1890s, many Americans modified outdoor games and sports so they could continue to enjoy them indoors. They created indoor versions of badminton and croquet, for example, and there were even archery sets for indoor use. Games that required skill, rather than luck, were especially popular, and this led to the development of a variety of target games, including this one for two to four players.

MATERIALS

several sheets of newspaper
*5 clean tuna fish cans (or cat food cans) with only
   the tops removed*
1 to 2 sheets of wrapping paper or construction paper
pencil
ruler
scissors
white glue
marking pen, black or red
pine board or thick cardboard, about 12-by-24 inches
5 thumbtacks or carpet tacks
hammer
*5 pebbles or dried beans for each player, and some
   extras*
adult helper

1. Spread several sheets of newspaper on your work surface and place the 5 empty cans on top.

2. With pencil and ruler, measure strips of wrapping paper or construction paper to fit around the outside of each can. Cut out the strips and fix them to the cans with a little white glue, as shown.

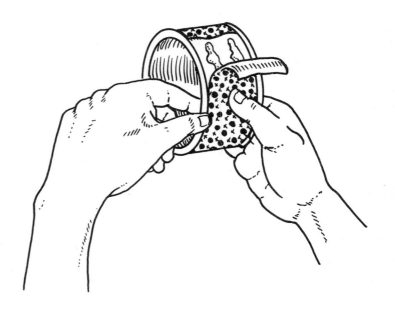

3. Use the marking pen to write the number 5 on the inside bottom of four of the cans and a 10 on the fifth can.

4. Arrange the cans on the board or cardboard with the 10-point target in the center, as shown in the drawing on the next page.

5. With an adult's help, use a hammer to tack the target cans in place. The sides of the four outer targets should touch the center target. Prop your target board against a piece of furniture or a stack of books and you're ready to play.

To Play

1. Two or three can play individually; if four play, divide into two teams.

2. Use any method you wish to see who goes first.

3. Practice a few times to establish a comfortable tossing line—a distance that makes scoring possible, but not too easy. Use extra pebbles to mark the line; once the line is marked, no player can cross it or reach over it.

4. Players take turns, with each player having 5 tosses. Fifty points are needed to win a round. If no one has 50 points after a round, the scores carry over to the next round.

A Great Time for Toys and Games

By the late 1800s, factories were producing great amounts of low-cost products, including dolls, toys, and games. Never before had people had such abundance and variety to choose from. As costs went down, more and more families could buy playthings for their children.

The first department stores had been established about 1860 and, by the 1890s, most had a special toy department. At the same time, companies like Sears and Montgomery Ward started the first mail order businesses, making it possible for people on the Western frontier to order toys and games for their children.

5. When a player or team reaches 50 points, the other players or team still must finish the round. If two players or teams end with 50 points or more, the highest score wins. In case of a tie, play one more round to determine a winner.

CHAPTER FOUR

WINTER

During the winter months, William Hobart spent much of his spare time in New York's Central Park. The enormous park, one of the first city parks in the nation, made a perfect winter playground for the city's growing population. As soon as the weather was cold enough, William and his friends joined hundreds of others ice skating on the lakes and ponds. When the Hobart family went ice skating together, William pushed Lucy around the ice on a chair he had rigged with runners from a sled.

Heavy snowfalls were not common in New York City, but there were several days when the family could rent a sleigh to ride through the park. There were often so many horse-drawn sleighs that a mounted policeman was needed to direct traffic. People also considered it quite adventurous to travel in a sleigh, rather than a carriage, to one of the many holiday parties.

SCIENTIFIC EXPERIMENTS

In school, William was fascinated by the study of crystals and his science teacher, Mr. Emblidge, suggested that he try growing crystals. William was especially pleased when he discovered he could grow his own rock candy crystals.

But a newspaper article suddenly made William more interested in invention than in scientific experiments. The article reported that two brothers named Duryea had tested a gasoline-powered automobile on the streets of Springfield, Massachusetts. William knew that European and American inventors had been trying for years to develop a "horseless carriage." Now the Duryea brothers had proved it was possible, although few people thought that motorcars would ever replace horses. William now began to dream of becoming a great inventor, finding ways to perfect the automobile. Once again, he turned to Mr. Emblidge, who showed him how to conduct some experiments with motion, including one in which he made a tin can roll across the floor by itself.

PROJECT THE ROLLING CAN

Throughout the late 1800s, inventors tried countless experiments in their efforts to develop the automobile. Many of the experiments involved trying to find the best source of power. Some worked with steam engines, others tried electric motors, and still others experimented with gasoline engines. The inventors also conducted experiments to help them understand the principles of motion and of stored energy, as you'll be doing in this activity. As you roll the can across the floor, the rubber band twists, storing up energy; when the energy is released, the can rolls the other way.

MATERIALS

coffee can, with both lids removed
metal file (if needed)
2 plastic coffee can lids
ruler
pencil
hole punch
long rubber band
scissors
bolt and nut (1 to 1½ inches long)
piece of string
adult helper (for filing)

1. Check to see if removing the lids left any sharp edges on the coffee cans. If there are any jagged points, ask your adult helper to help you use a file to smooth those spots.

2. With ruler and pencil make two marks about 3 inches apart on the middle of each plastic lid.

3. Use the hole punch to make a hole through each mark on both lids.

4. Cut the rubber band with scissors. Push each end of the rubber band through the holes in the top of one lid.

5. Cross the ends of the rubber band, forming an X, with the X at the halfway point, as shown in the illustration.

6. Use a small piece of string to tie the nut and bolt to the middle of the rubber band, at the X, as shown.

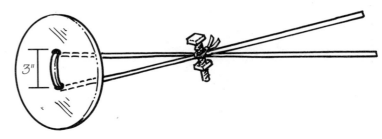

The Horseless Carriage

Although the Duryea brothers had test-ed an automobile in September 1893, it took many inventors several years to make a workable motorcar. Many peo-ple disliked the noisy vehicles because they frightened horses. They scared a few people as well—in some towns, drivers were required to have someone walk in front of the automobile to warn people of its approach! By 1900, there were about 8,000 motorcars in the entire country. But there were 18,000,000 horses and mules that peo-ple continued to rely on for transporta-tion. A leading magazine predicted that "the horseless carriage will never be as common as the bicycle."

7. Place the lid on the can, with the rubber band and the nut and bolt inside the can.

8. Push the two ends of the rubber band through the holes in the other lid, this time from the bottom of the lid. Hold the ends of the rubber band to keep them from slipping out and place the lid on the can. Make sure the rubber band forms an X inside the can.

9. Tie the ends of the rub-ber band together in a firm double knot. Your can is now ready to roll.

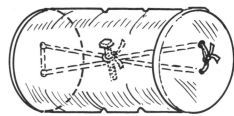

10. Roll the can across the floor. (A rug or carpet will provide better traction than bare wood or tile.) When the can stops rolling, the stored-up energy in the wound rubber band will cause the can to roll back to you.

 **ROCK CANDY CRYSTALS**

Rock candy was one of the most popular sweets of the late 1800s. It was also one of the least expensive. A penny bag could last an entire day. Many kids preferred to make their own candy crystals, following the same recipe you'll be using. While traditional rock candy was always white, you can add color for variety.

INGREDIENTS

1½ cups water

3 cups sugar

food coloring, any 2 or 3 colors (optional)

EQUIPMENT

small saucepan

mixing spoon

3 small jars or glasses

about 30 inches of clean string

scissors

3 pencils or thin dowels

3 paper clips or metal washers

adult helper

MAKES

4 to 6 snack servings

1. Pour the water into the saucepan and, with an adult's help, bring it to a boil over medium-high heat.

2. Add the sugar a little at a time, stirring constantly. If the sugar water starts to boil over, lower the heat to medium.

3. Continue adding sugar and stirring until you have a smooth, clear syrup. Turn off the heat and let the syrup cool for 10 to 15 minutes.

4. While the syrup cools, tie a piece of string to the middle of a pencil or dowel. Lay the pencil across a jar or glass. Measure and cut the string to reach just to the bottom of the glass or jar. Tie a clean paper clip or washer to the end of the string, as shown, to keep the string straight.

5. Repeat step 4 to set up the other two jars or glasses with weighted strings.

6. When the syrup has cooled to lukewarm, carefully pour roughly equal amounts into each jar or glass.

7. If you wish, add a few drops of food coloring to two jars and leave the third one white. You might make red, white, and blue crystals, for example, or any other colors you wish.

8. Store the jars in a warm place for about one week. Check the jars every day. By the second day, you should see crystals forming along the string. A crust usually forms on the surface of the syrup. Use the handle of a mixing spoon to gen-

tly poke through the crust, but don't stir it. Breaking the crust allows the syrup to evaporate faster, which speeds the formation of crystals, but stirring or shaking the syrup disturbs the process.

9. After seven days, if the syrup hasn't evaporated completely and crystals still seem to be forming, let the jars sit for another day or two

10. When no more crystals are forming—or you can't wait any longer to sample your creation—remove the strings from the jars, untie the pencils, and put your rock candy crystals in a candy dish. (You can leave the crystals on the strings or pull them off.) The crystals will harden more as they dry, and you'll have a good idea why this was called *rock* candy.

PRESENTS FOR LUCY

One day in early December, when Lucy and her nanny Margaret were walking to the park, a runaway horse and carriage careened into a group of people. No one was seriously hurt, but Margaret and Lucy were thrown to the ground. They suffered cuts and bruises, and Lucy's ankle was sprained. Although runaway horses were a serious problem in America's growing cities, they did not often cause serious injuries.

While Lucy recovered, William brought her a present each day. He made a small folding fan for her to use when she dressed up like Mother, and drew a series of mazes because he knew she liked to solve puzzles. He also made a snowfall jar, copying the snow globes sold in stores, which had become one of the most popular toys of the 1890s.

The snowfall jar gave William the idea for a scientific experiment. His parents had given him a Kodak camera and he decided to try to use it to make photographs of snowflakes. The experiment did not work well because the photos were too blurred. Once again Mr. Emblidge helped him by showing him how to make impressions of snowflakes on a glass plate. This experiment was much more successful.

PROJECT SNOWFLAKE IMPRESSIONS

All snowflakes are six-sided ice crystals, which are formed into an endless variety of shapes. It is often said that no two snowflakes are exactly alike. To make a record that gives an idea of the variety and beauty of these crystals, try this simple activity.

MATERIALS

picture frame with glass, about 8-by-10 inches
can of hairspray or artist's fixative (available
    wherever art supplies are sold)
falling snow
magnifying glass

1. When you're pretty sure that a snowfall is coming, place the glass frame and the spray can in a safe place outdoors or in the freezer compartment of your refrigerator. Chill the materials for about an hour.

2. When the snow is falling, take the glass and spray can outdoors. Hold the can about 10 inches from the glass and spray it with a quick sweeping motion. Spray from side to side once, then up and down. Use very little spray—a second or two is all you need.

3. Collect some snowflakes on the sprayed surface.

4. Take the glass indoors and let it dry at room temperature for 15 to 20 minutes. Check your results with a magnifying glass. You should have a record of some remarkable crystals of ice.

PROJECT SNOWFALL JAR

No one knows who invented the snow globe, but this simple device has been giving pleasure to people of all ages for more than a hundred years. The factory-produced globes are made with a heavy glass ball, but you can make a very good imitation using a water-tight jar. A small jar, like those used for baby food, works well, but a slightly larger jar, such as a jam jar, is even easier to work with. For your snow scene, use a small Christmas tree ornament, such as a snowman or a Santa, or you might prefer to make a "natural" scene with a small evergreen branch shaped like a miniature tree.

MATERIALS

several sheets of newspaper
small water-tight jar and lid, with label removed
green acrylic paint
white acrylic paint (optional)
small paintbrush
piece of self-hardening clay (2 to 4 ounces should be plenty)
water-resistant glue
small ornament, branch, or other object for your winter scene
distilled water (available at supermarkets)
2 to 4 tablespoons of glitter, white or silver
narrow red or plaid ribbon, about 18 inches

1. Spread several sheets of newspaper on your work surface.

2. Test the jar by filling it with water, screwing the lid on tight, and letting the jar sit, lid side down, for a few minutes to make sure it doesn't leak.

3. Paint the outside of the lid green. You'll probably need 2 or 3 coats; let the paint dry for 15 to 20 minutes between coats (check the directions on the tube or bottle).

4. Place a little water-resistant glue on the inside of the jar lid and work a piece of self-hardening clay into the lid. This will form the "ground" for your snow scene.

5. Press the ornament or other object firmly into the clay. If necessary, use a little water-resistant glue to fix it in place.

Photography and Snowflakes

Early cameras were bulky and difficult to use. A portrait, for example, required the subject to stay perfectly still for several minutes while an image was recorded on a glass plate. In the late 1880s, George Eastman developed roll film and an easy-to-use camera he called the Kodak. From that time on, people could take pictures without lots of expensive equipment.

Another pioneer of photography was Wilson Bentley, who used special lenses to photograph snowflakes. Between 1880 and 1930, Bentley made more than 4,000 snowflake photographs, mostly near his home in Vermont. Not surprisingly, Bentley became known as the "snowflake man," and his photographs are still used in the study of snow crystals.

6. If necessary, paint the clay white to look like snow-covered ground.

7. Fill the jar to the top with distilled water. Add two tablespoons of glitter.

8. Carefully put on the lid and tighten it firmly. Turn the jar right side up, shake it gently, then turn it over and watch the snow fall!

9. If necessary, add a little more glitter until you have the kind of snowfall you want. Tie the ribbon with a bow around the lid as a finishing touch.

PROJECT VICTORIAN FOLDING FAN

A folding fan was an essential part of every fashionable woman's attire in the 1890s, along with her gloves and her hat. The fan not only provided a cooling breeze when needed, but it was also a useful prop for conversation. It was not polite for a lady to point, for example, but she could indicate direction with her fan without attracting attention. In a similar way, an open fan could serve as a screen behind which a Victorian lady could whisper to her companion. When young girls played "dress up," they practiced the many ways to use the folding fan.

MATERIALS

3 sheets of poster board in 3 different colors
ruler
pencil
scissors
hole punch
crayons or colored pencils
brass paper fastener
yarn or twine, any color, about 38 inches

1. On one piece of poster board, use ruler and pencil to copy the drawing for a single fan blade, about 7 inches long. Notice that the blade tapers a little, from a width of 1¾ inches at the top to 1½ inches at the bottom, as shown. Cut out the fan blade with scissors. Round off the corners on both the top and bottom, as shown in the drawing.

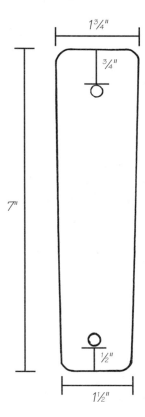

2. Use this first blade as a pattern to make nine more blades: Place the blade on a piece of poster board, trace around it with pencil, then cut out the new blade. Make three blades in each of your three colors.

3. Use a hole punch to make holes in the top and bottom of all ten blades. Make the top holes about ¾ inch from the top edge and the bottom holes ½ inch from the bottom edge.

4. Use crayons or colored pencils to add a decoration to each blade. Draw a different design on each set of colors.

5. Place the blades in a stack, alternating the colors. Push a brass paper fastener through all the bottom holes. Spread the prongs of the fastener.

6. Tie one end of the yarn or twine to the top hole of the first blade, then string the yarn through the top holes of the other blades. Open the fan and adjust the yarn or twine so that the blades are spaced evenly. Tie the end of the yarn to the last blade and trim off any extra with scissors. Your folding fan is now ready for Victorian social occasions.

MAZE GREETING CARD

Mazes are great fun to make and they have a variety of uses. In the 1890s, for example, mazes were used as parlor games, with individuals or teams trying to outdo one another either in creating mazes or in solving them. In this project, you'll make a maze greeting card. These can be used as intriguing party invitations or as cards for special occasions, like birthdays or Valentine's Day.

There are a few simple rules to follow for building a maze. It's important to follow these rules so that you don't end up with a maze that can't be solved!

MATERIALS
scrap paper
pencil
ruler
1 sheet of sturdy white paper, about 7-by-9 inches
scissors
pen
envelope

1. Work out your maze on scrap paper first, then copy it on good paper for mailing.

2. Begin by drawing a center goal. This can be a picture, a greeting or, for a party invitation, the information about the party. Draw a wall around this center square with a small open space, known as a "door."

3. Draw a second wall around the first, again with one door. Place the door wherever you wish. The space between the two walls is called a

The Amazing Maze Craze

Mazes had been popular in Europe for hundreds of years, and mazes constructed in gardens were of particular interest. In the 1880s, wealthy Americans suddenly became interested in European garden mazes. Some sent their gardeners to England or France to study their construction. The walls of garden mazes were hedges—bushes that were so high and thick that people couldn't see through them or crawl through them. Just as in drawn mazes, the garden mazes contained any number of blank walls as well as a correct door in each wall. Once a visitor reached the center square—which was not always in the center—there was still the problem of getting back out!

The maze craze continued into the early 1900s.

"hall" or "alley." At some point in this hall, draw a line between the two walls, creating a "blank wall," as shown in the illustration.

4. Make a third wall, remembering to include a door and a blank wall. Make as many additional walls as you wish. Now that you know how to do it, try making more mazes. Try having two or three goals to reach instead of one, or try working with circles instead of squares.

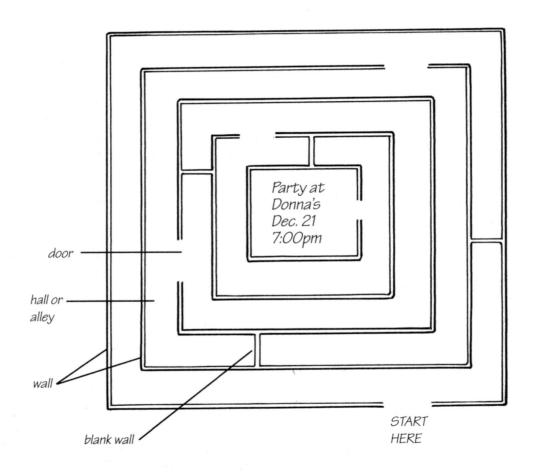

door

hall or alley

wall

blank wall

Party at Donna's Dec. 21 7:00pm

START HERE

THE HOLIDAY SEASON

For William, one of the great pleasures of the holiday season was sharing the fun and excitement with his sister Lucy. For one adventure, he took her for a ride on a horse-drawn trolley car to New York's main shopping district near Fifth Avenue. They made their way through the crowds of shoppers to the big department stores where Lucy gazed in wonder at the beautiful Christmas scenes in the store windows. She especially loved the scenes of Santa Claus flying through the night sky in his toy-laden sleigh.

The holidays were also the season for entertaining, and wealthy Victorians competed with one another to see who could give the most elegant dinner parties. Although Mr. and Mrs. Hobart felt obligated to attend some of these parties, they preferred to make Christmas a quiet family time with only a few relatives. The family worked together to make ornaments and decorate the tree. Mrs. Bentley invited William and Lucy into the kitchen, where she showed

William how to make delicious ice cream sundaes out of candy canes. She also let him cut up the pieces of fruit for the holiday punch.

PROJECT HOLIDAY FRUIT PUNCH

Dinner parties were the favorite way of entertaining in the 1890s. A dinner might include forty guests, last for three hours or more, and consist of at least four courses but usually more. While many hostesses served a different wine with each course, punch was also a popular beverage. A hot punch, or "negus," was made with wine and spices. A cold punch, like the one you'll make, was poured over a big block of ice in a large punch bowl. At a really lavish Victorian party, the punch would be served in a fountain. You won't need a fountain! And, if you want to make a smaller batch of punch, simply divide the ingredients in half.

INGREDIENTS

1 cup water
½ cup sugar
2 quarts cranberry-juice cocktail
1 cup orange juice
2 lemons
1 orange
4 or 5 cocktail cherries
1 quart ginger ale (refrigerated)
3 or 4 trays of ice cubes, or large cake of ice that will fit in your punch bowl

EQUIPMENT

small saucepan
mixing spoon
large pitcher
paring knife (to be used with an adult)
cutting board
punch bowl with ladle
adult helper

MAKES

15 to 20 servings

1. Pour the water into a small saucepan and add the sugar. With an adult's help, heat the sugar-water to boiling over medium-high heat, stirring frequently.

2. Continue to boil gently until all the sugar has dissolved. Turn off the heat and let the sugar syrup cool for about 10 minutes.

3. While the sugar syrup cools, pour the cranberry-juice cocktail and orange juice into a large pitcher.

4. Ask the adult to help you use a paring knife to cut 1 lemon and an orange into thin slices. Cut 4 or 5 cocktail cherries in half. Set the fruits aside on the cutting board.

5. Cut the other lemon in half and squeeze the juice into the pitcher with the cranberry-juice cocktail and orange juice.

6. Stir in the sugar syrup.

7. When you're ready to serve, place the ice in the punch bowl and pour in the contents of the juice pitcher. Add the ginger ale by pouring it slowly down the inside of the bowl—not directly over the ice.

8. Place a half cherry and a lemon slice on top of an orange slice and float it in the punch. Make several more of these stacks to float in the bowl.

The "Gay" Nineties

The decade of the 1890s became known as the "Gay Nineties" because of the endless rounds of dinner parties and other forms of entertainment enjoyed by wealthy Americans. People who were not part of society's upper classes enjoyed reading about the elegant affairs. A dinner party given by a famous New York hostess, like Mrs. Astor or Mrs. Vanderbilt, was reported on the front page of the newspapers. People also liked to read about the many foreign dignitaries who attended—princes and princesses, dukes and duchesses, lords and ladies.

Many Americans, including some of the wealthy, said that these parties were a terrible waste of money, especially when so many people lacked basic necessities. Some of the richest businessmen gave away most of their fortunes. Andrew Carnegie, for instance, gave four hundred million dollars to worthy causes, almost half of it to build free public libraries.

PROJECT CANDY CANE SUNDAES

At Victorian dinner parties, every dish was carefully prepared not only for taste, but for appearance as well. A bit of garnish, like a sprig of parsley or a slice of lemon might be all that was needed to make a serving dish attractive, or a bowl of fruit might be made into a beautiful fruit sculpture that also served as the table centerpiece. Desserts, too, had to look good and taste delicious. That's what you'll achieve in this recipe by combining color with flavor.

INGREDIENTS

2 to 4 peppermint candy canes
1 cup water
½ cup sugar
¼ cup light corn syrup
2 tablespoons water
1 tablespoon cornstarch
red and green food coloring
1 cup whipping cream
1 quart ice cream, vanilla or chocolate, or 1 pint
  of each
red or green cocktail cherries (optional)

EQUIPMENT

medium-size saucepan
mixing spoon
small dish
2 small pitchers
medium-size mixing bowl
egg beater
dessert dishes
ice cream scoop
adult helper

MAKES

4 to 6 servings

1. Break enough peppermint candy canes into small pieces to make ½ cup. (You'll find it easiest to crush the candy canes while they're still in their wrapping, then pour the pieces into a measuring cup.)

2. Put the crushed candy in a saucepan and add 1 cup of water, the sugar, and the light corn syrup. Stir and, with an adult's help, bring the mixture to a boil over medium-high heat.

3. Reduce the heat and let the mixture simmer until the candy has dissolved completely. Stir frequently.

4. Mix 2 tablespoons of water with the cornstarch in a small dish or measuring cup. Stir until the cornstarch has dissolved.

5. Add the cornstarch to the peppermint mixture. Stir well and simmer until the mixture thickens into syrup.

6. Pour half the peppermint syrup into each of the two pitchers. Stir a few drops of red food coloring into one pitcher and a few drops of green food coloring into the other.

7. While the syrup cools, pour the cream into the mixing bowl. Beat it with an egg beater until the whipped cream forms peaks.

8. When you're ready to serve, scoop ice cream into dessert dishes, add syrup, a little whipped cream, and a red or green cherry, if desired. Mix colors to make each sundae attractive. Chocolate ice cream, for example, goes better with red syrup than with green; vanilla ice cream looks appealing with either color. Use the cocktail cherries for an additional splash of color and you have a true Victorian-style dessert!

PROJECT EASY-TO-MAKE ORNAMENTS

Most Americans in the 1890s regarded Christmas as a quiet family day. Many families waited until Christmas Eve to decorate their trees, and they often preferred ornaments they had made themselves to factory-made decorations. This tradition continues today and people find they remember best the ornaments that were handmade. You'll find that the ornaments in this project are not only easy and fun to make, but they're also a good way to make use of scrap materials. Make several ornaments of each design in varying colors and create your own designs as well.

MATERIAL
scraps of poster board, different colors, 6-by-4 inches or larger
pencil
ruler
pinking shears
scissors
hole punch
scraps of yarn, each at least 20 inches long, red, and green, or any other colors
white glue or craft glue
string or thread

1. Place a piece of poster board on your work surface and copy one of the designs shown here lightly in pencil.

2. Cut out the shape with pinking shears. You might find it easier to cut the basic design with scissors and then trim the edges with the pinking shears.

3. For the candy cane, use a long piece of red yarn (about 36 inches). Glue one end to the bottom of the cane, then wind it around the full length of the cane, as shown. The jagged edges will hold the yarn in place. When you've covered the pattern, cut the yarn, and glue the end to the poster board.

4. Use a hole punch to make a hole in the curve of the cane. Run a piece of string or thread through the hole and tie it in a double knot for hanging.

5. For other patterns, like the fish or tree, use the hole punch to make holes about an inch apart around the edges, as shown. Choose a color of yarn that goes well with the poster board color, and weave it in and out of the holes.

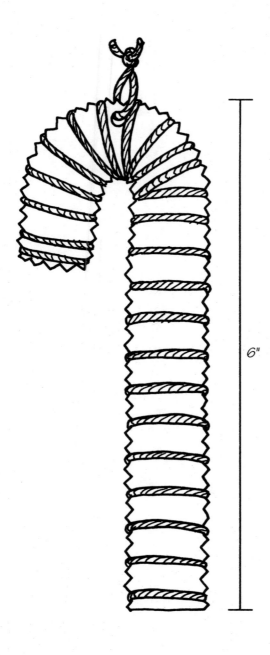

6″

6. Tie the ends of the yarn in a loop and then a double knot for hanging.

7. Cut out more patterns, or design your own, and experiment with different color combinations. Hang the ornaments individually, or string several together to hang from a Christmas tree, a doorway, or a window.

GLOSSARY

alley   In a maze, the open area between two walls, also called a "hall."

beach glass   Pieces of glass that have been worn smooth by the action of wind, waves, and sand.

bell jar   A large glass dome used by well-to-do Victorians to display dried flower arrangements.

blank wall   A dead-end in a maze.

casing   The upper part of a drawstring bag that holds the string or cord.

cat   A tie game in tic-tac-toe and tic-tac-taw.

Central Park   Built in New York City in the nineteenth century, it is one of the largest and most beautiful city parks in the world.

decoupage   The craft of covering a box or other object with small pictures, then applying several coats of varnish, from the French word *découper*, meaning to cut up.

diaphragm   A thin disk on a telephone or microphone that transfers electrical impulses into sound by its vibrations.

door The open space in the wall of a maze.

Easter Parade The name given to the Easter procession of fancy carriages in New York City in the 1890s.

Gay Nineties The name used to describe the 1890s because of the lavish and costly forms of entertainment enjoyed by only the wealthiest people.

graham crackers Developed by Dr. Sylvester Graham in the mid 1800s to provide a healthier form of flour in the American diet.

hall The open area between the walls of a maze, also called an "alley."

horseless carriage One of the names used to describe early automobiles.

immigrants People who move to a country from another part of the world.

industrial schools Schools first developed in the 1890s to provide students with job skills as well as training in traditional subjects like reading and math.

knuckle down To shoot a marble correctly, with one knuckle on the ground.

lazy-daisy stitch A long embroidery stitch made by creating a loop of floss, then anchoring the other end of the loop with a small stitch.

negus   A hot punch made with wine and spices.

piecework   The method of paying sweatshop workers by the number of pieces completed, rather than by the hour.

Polish checkers   A form of checkers played on a board with 100 squares, rather than 64, in which the kings have much more flexibility.

Polish paper cutouts   A beautiful art form of intricate paper patterns developed by Polish farm families in the 1800s.

R.S.V.P.   The initials on an invitation asking for an answer to the invitation, from the French phrase "*Répondez, s'il vous plait* (ray-PON-day SEE voo-PLAY), meaning "please respond" or reply.

running stitch   A straight sewing stitch used to sew a seam.

sailors' valentines   Small hinged boxes containing shell art, made by sailors at sea and given as presents.

scraps   Small pictures cut from magazines, newspapers, or special sheets of scraps.

scrimshaw   The sailors' art of carving beautiful pictures on a piece of ivory, such as a whale's tooth.

settlement houses Establishments created in the late 1800s to help immigrants adjust to life in America.

speaking telegraph A name used to describe the earliest form of the telephone.

static discharge A spark of light created by the movement between positive and negative charges, as in lightning.

sweatshops Factories or tenement apartments where people worked long hours, for very low wages, under unhealthy conditions.

taw In the game of marbles, a player's special shooting marble.

tenements Crowded, unsanitary apartments where many poor people were forced to live because they could not afford better housing.

Victorian Age The term used to describe the period from about 1840 to 1900 in England and the United States, during the reign of England's Queen Victoria.

wax-resist A method of dyeing in which areas covered with wax resist—or don't receive—the dye.

wycinanka ludowa (vi-chee-NON-kah loo-DOH-vah) A Polish term meaning "folk paper art," referring to Polish paper cutouts.

BIBLIOGRAPHY

Suzanne I. Barchers and Patricia C. Marden. *Cooking Up U.S. History: Recipes and Research to Share with Children.* Chicago: Teachers Ideas Press, 1991.

Josef and Dorothy Berger, eds. *Diary of America.* New York: Simon & Schuster, 1957.

Joseph Byron. *New York Life at the Turn of the Century in Photographs.* New York: Dover Publications, 1985.

Cobblestone, The History Magazine for Young People. 30 Grove Street, Peterborough, NH 03458.
    Children's Toys, December 1986
    America's Folk Art, August 1991

Marshall Davidson. *Life in America,* 2 vols. Boston: Houghton Mifflin, 1951.

Gwen Evrard. *Homespun Crafts from Scraps.* New York: New Century Publishers, 1982.

Phyllis Fiarotta. S*nips and Snails and Walnut Whales: Nature Crafts for Children.* New York: Workman Publishing, 1975.

John Grafton. *New York in the Nineteenth Century.* New York: Dover Publications, 1980.

David C. King. *The Age of Technology: 19th Century American Inventors.* Carlisle, MA: Discovery Enterprises, 1997.

John A. Kouwenhoven. *Adventures of America, 1857–1900: A Pictorial Record from Harper's Weekly.* New York: Harper & Brothers, 1938.

Susan Milord. *Adventures in Art: Art and Craft Experiences for 7- to 14-Year-Olds.* Charlotte, VT: Williamson Publishing, 1990.

Wilma Lord Perkins. *The All New Fannie Farmer Boston Cooking School Cookbook.* Boston: Little, Brown, 1936.

Susan Purdy. *Festivals for You to Celebrate: Facts, Activities, and Crafts.* Philadelphia: J.B. Lippincott, 1969.

Carl P. Stirn. *Turn of the Century Dolls, Toys and Games: The Complete Illustrated Carl P. Stirn Catalog for 1893.* New York: Dover Publications, 1990.

Laura Wilson. *Daily Life in a Victorian House.* New York: Puffin Books, 1993.

INDEX